Who Are You Online?

Visit WhooRu on the Internet: http://www.whooru.com/

Visit Aaron Francesconi on the Internet: http://www.aaronfrancesconi.com/

EAN 13: 9781450516099
ISBN 10: 1450516092

Who Are You Online?

Why It Matters and What You Can Do About It!

Aaron Francesconi, M.B.A

For Carol, Nickey, Aria, and Clarissa

May you always reach for the stars

Always and Forever

About the Author

Aaron has always been involved with technology. At the age of 12, Aaron bought his first computer, a used Commodore 128, with $500 he saved from working a paper route.

While Aaron was finishing high school, he started learning how to use web technologies. Late in 1994, Aaron started creating personal websites for individuals. Aaron has built web sites for individuals, organizations, businesses, and the academic, private, and government sectors.

In March 2008, Aaron launched his company, WhooRu.com. WhooRu's mission is to help people control how they appear on the Internet. Through proactive measures anyone can benefit from controlling how they appear on the Internet, both professionally and personally.

Aaron is currently the Web Services Manager for Utah Retirement Systems, the CEO of WhooRu.com, and the author of this book, *Who Are You Online?: Why It Matters and What You Can Do About It!* In his spare time, he likes to sleep.

Aaron has a Masters of Business Administration (MBA) degree from Weber State University and a Bachelors of Music in Vocal Performance from Idaho State University.

Contents at a Glance

Acknowledgements

No man is an island. Without several people along the way, this book would have not been possible.

First and foremost, I thank God for giving me talent, inspiration, motivation, and determination. In the future, I would like to thank God for several more material possessions.

My soulmate, Carol for helping me at every step of the way. In partikular her editing skillz, (so if you see something amiss....) Without her faith in me, I would have probably given up a long time ago. Either that or I would have been found in a Howard Hughes like state. She is my number one fan and I am her number one devotee. You complete me.

My children, with all their silly jokes, (knock knock, who's there, elliphino) for allowing their dad the time to write this book and sometimes even get some sleep.

My family for believing in my capabilities.

Ben Folds and Allison Krauss for providing the soundtrack to the book.

My brother, Anthony, for seeing the promise of what I was trying to do.

My dog, Sconi, a Boston Terrier known for his capability to clear a room in two seconds. He died while I was writing this book. He reminded me of the value of man's best friend.

The people throughout my life who helped shape me into who I am today.

My friends from Pocatello, Idaho for giving me great memories and stories to tell for the rest of my life.

The TCA, PSAA, and the 20th Ward.

The Ransom family for helping someone they didn't have to and forever impacting my life.

My friend, Anna Schultz, for her fantastic design work on the cover of the book.

But definitely, I *do not* want to thank Colonel Sanders, with his beady little eyes and his addictive ingredients in his chicken.

Table of Contents

Part II – What You Can Do About It!

PART I

WHY IT MATTERS

CHAPTER ONE

THE ABSENCE OF PRIVACY
ON A GLOBAL SCALE

"The Internet is becoming the town square for the global village of tomorrow."

—Bill Gates, Founder of Microsoft

Humanity is in the beginning stages of an information revolution which is dramatically changing the way people learn about each other. If a person needs to know something about someone, they no longer turn to a private investigator, they turn to their favorite search engine. This socially accepted behavior has introduced a new and unique problem that humankind has not yet seen or dealt with before: the absence of privacy on a global scale.

The Internet has allowed the average person to find out about people as though they were next door neighbors, from thousands of miles away behind the warm glow of a computer monitor. In turn, they are judging people based on very limited information assembled from the Internet, regardless of the truthfulness of that information. In a 2006 study by ExecuNet, 77% of executive recruiters use the

Internet to research job candidates. Thirty-five percent of candidates were eliminated based on the search results. That was in 2006 and its only gotten worse since.

Who Are You Online?: Why It Matters and What You Can Do About It! is a how-to guide for people navigating the perfect social storm created by the Internet. Rather than seeing the Internet as a problem, people need to use the Internet as an opportunity to achieve goals such as career aspirations, new relationships, protection from slander, and educational goals amongst others. *Who Are You Online?: Why It Matters and What You Can Do About It!* shows you the way.

THE INTERNET AND ITS TRANSFORMING EFFECT ON OUR LIVES

Ladies and Gentlemen, stop the presses. I have an earth-shattering proclamation for you. It's the most important bit of knowledge you will ever learn in your lifetime. Without further ado. Can I get a drum roll please? Dadadadadadada.... It's official, the Internet is here to stay!

Impossible! Inconceivable!! He's out of his gourd!!! I paid $39.99 for this book and this is what I learned!!!! Before you run back to your local bookstore, I promise, it gets better. This tidbit of information is the premise on which this book is written. If the Internet were going away, who would care about who they were online. The Internet is here to stay is the one and only simple truth about the Internet.

"The Internet is here to stay" conveys exactly how permanent of a fixture the Internet has quickly become in our lives. Not long before the dotcom crash of 2000, people were predicting the downfall of the Internet. While many of pets.coms' failed, (sites which really had no chance of survival), the critics of the Internet were wrong. The Internet hasn't gone anywhere and rather, it is thriving. It's getting harder and harder to name areas where the Internet can't impact your life. Need to eat? Order a pizza at the click of a button. Looking for love? Look no further than online dating sites. Need to check references on a baby-sitter? Become their friend on Facebook.   Need to get tickets to a concert? Skip the box office and go online. Need to find a rare part for a 1957 Chevrolet Bel-Aire Convertible? View the inventory of a thousand junk yards from your garage. When you really think about it, when was the last time you used a travel agent, the phone book, the card catalogue system at the library, or heaven forbid an encyclopedia? Chances are, it has been a long time.

How many times a day do you access the Internet? Furthermore, how many times do you think, "I need to look that up on the Internet"? If you don't know how to use the Internet, how often are you told to "look it up online" or to "send an e-mail" instead of calling them? No matter who you are, you can't escape the reach of the Internet.

There is no debate as to whether or not the Internet will survive in the 21st century. The real question is, will you survive the 21st century? You might be asking yourself, "Why wouldn't I survive the 21st century?" Well the long and short of it is the ability to survive and thrive with life-changing technology. Life is changing rapidly now and from the looks of things, we have barely seen the tip of the iceberg.   As an example of the speed of change, modern innovations such as Internet browsers, MP3 players, GPS units, and digital cameras didn't exist in 1990 and now it's hard to imagine life without them.

With any innovation, it changes our lives. Most of the time, change is quite positive. With digital cameras, we can take as many pictures as we want to without incurring the expenses like we used to with regular film cameras. Furthermore, at the same time we don't have to develop pictures anymore. We can simply e-mail them. Yet at the same time, technology has made it easier for people who commit heinous acts to work more efficiently. Scam artists, identity thieves, pedophiles, stalkers, robbers, all have access to the Internet. With a powerful tool like the Internet, you are going to find there is the ability to do great things, while at the same time the Internet can be used for insidious purposes. When it comes to our personal lives, the Internet can be used to showcase who we are and what we desire out of this life. The challenge for this generation and the ones to come is to harness the power of the Internet and use it for good.

The Internet has been one of mankind's greatest innovations. As a convergence of multiple technologies, the Internet has amazing capabilities and carries with it the promise of transforming all aspects of interaction with other people. The Internet has brought with it a whole new range of expected skills a person has to have on the job. As the Internet generation moves further into the workforce, the skills required to use the technology will be an essential job skill. Knowledge workers will need to use the Internet to find information on the things they are working on. Marketers will need the Internet to track trends and target niche markets. HR specialists will use the Internet to profile and do background checks on job candidates.

The largest impact to your life in the 21st century will be the interconnectivity the Internet brings. The interconnectivity of the Internet has changed the rules of most aspects of our lives. In order to be a part of the evolving society, adaptation is required to utilize the tools being built for everyday living. Failure to adapt and use the Internet will be very detrimental to a career which will depend on use of the Internet. To be able to adapt, you will need to learn new skills which show your ability to interact with other people in a digital manner.

From a social point of view, the Internet is transforming our lives in many positive ways. People are able to find love who previously could not. People are able to gather with groups of people who share their viewpoints as well as read opposing viewpoints. Acceptance of using the Internet for social means is growing. From dating to using it as a gathering place for friends, society is becoming more accepting of the Internet as a tool for social interaction.

Back in 1997 when I met my wife online, I was embarrassed to admit that we met on AOL. In fact, we told a lot of people we met at church. When they inevitably would press for more information, we feigned embarrassment and admitted to meeting online.   Of course, we were very quick to point out we never dated over the Internet. That being said, the mere fact that we met on the Internet raised a few eyebrows and questions about building a relationship with someone over the Internet.   At the time we were pioneers. We paved the way for future generations to meet online. Now, everyone and their dog seem to be meeting online. (Seriously, have you tried looking for your next puppy online? There are puppy websites everywhere.) The social stigma about the using the Internet for everything is leaving as rapidly as online dating sites (and puppy sites) are appearing.

While the social use of the Internet has brought about positive changes for social interaction, it has also brought out a darker side of interaction. As people use the Internet for social interaction, many of their activities are recorded for later consumption. That type of social interaction would be fine if what you wrote on the Internet was only seen by the intended parties. However, the Internet is becoming a massive reference check station for anyone who cares to use it in that fashion. With relative anonymity, you can search for anything and everyone you want to, unless of course, you live in a country which filters Internet searches.

Nevertheless, as individuals turn to the Internet for information more and more in their personal lives, they are going to find information about other people on the Internet. Increasingly as people you interact with find information about you they are using it to make decisions about you. The decisions people are making range from whether or not you get an interview, to whether or not you are marriage material. Often when people have limited information about you, they will tend to make the wrong decision. Have you ever been asked in an in a job interview, "So is it difficult being Jewish?" With a follow up question regarding your sexuality, "do your orthodox parents know you are gay?" Chances are you haven't been asked those questions and for a reason. Not only do they have no bearing whatsoever on how you will perform on the job, they are discriminatory and illegal (at least in more developed countries). The reason you haven't been asked these questions are because they could be the basis for a lawsuit against the company, and yet people will publish this information about themselves willingly and all the time.   Yet they still wonder why they can't seem to figure out why the trail went cold on a job opportunity or why people eventually find out about some of the information they like to keep private in work settings.

THE UNINTENTIONAL LOSS OF PRIVACY

We, as a people, are just barely learning how to use the Internet and our new found interconnectivity. Most people see the Internet as a means of getting shopping done or transacting business. Socially, we have started communicating with each other over social networking web sites. As an information gathering tool, we have started to use the Internet to find out information about things we don't know. For instance, companies are starting to monitor blogging to see how their product is perceived. But we still have just scratched the surface of what is possible in an interconnected world.

Imagine the possibilities of the world of tomorrow in an Internet connected home. Imagine how great it would be if your home could tell you what you needed to buy at the grocery store. Or better still, your home could analyze what you tend to use in a two week period and could arrange for the grocery store to deliver the items you need for the next two weeks. Or even better yet, your home could do diet planning for you. It could be connected to your toilet and analyze your nutritional needs. Your home could figure out the optimal diet for you to maintain your perfect weight. And what if your dentist could talk with your home and see how often you really floss? (OK, when did this turn into a scenario from hell?) While this is all technically possible today, the largest deterrent to this scenario is not the expense required, it's the potential loss of privacy. There would be high incentive for criminals to hack your home. If they could hack your home, all of the sensors required for your home to be fully interactive with you could be used to monitor you. Imagine if someone could listen into everything that was said in your house. What if your employer could monitor everything you said about them and then act on what they heard and saw? It wouldn't take long for most of us to be out a job except for me, because I never bad mouth anybody when I am at home.

Now imagine if you will, that it didn't take an act of crime for someone to spy in on your home to see what and who you are in your private life. What if you could choose to publicly display your life for your friends and family, or anyone else who stumbles across your Internet feed? Would you broadcast your home life over the Internet? Of course you wouldn't. Your home is your sanctuary. Putting what goes on in our home life in the Internet makes as little sense as putting our private lives on public display. Yet, putting private lives on public display is exactly what many people are doing as they create personal blogs, online journals, and haphazardly use social networking sites like Facebook and MySpace. What's worse is people aren't stopping at documenting and posting the lurid details of their lives, they're taking us all under at the same time. By posting details of their life, if you happen to be one of their friends or family members, you can get included in their postings.

So why is this happening? Surely people are aware of the consequences of their actions. In most cases, people are aware what they do can have repercussions. People are smart enough to know what to say in front of their employer and what not to say in front of their employer. Those of us who don't know how to behave are taught by having an employer fire or likewise reprimand them. The problem with the Internet is all of us are still adapting to the technology. As we adapt to technology, we will experiment with the technology to see how it can solve the problems we all face every day. With experimentation, we will make mistakes from time to time, which is how a lot of us learn. The biggest mistake private individuals have made to date is thinking that they are anonymous on the Internet.

ANONYMITY ON THE INTERNET

The belief that people think they are anonymous on the Internet is fueled by people thinking the Internet is vast and huge, and they are a small player on the Internet. Further, the belief is backed up by the thought that only the people they want to see their information have access or would seek out that information.

Yet, the belief that you can keep yourself off the Internet is a myth. There are too many players who can contribute to the knowledge that can be found on the Internet. You, your friends, your enemies, your family members, the organizations you associate with have the ability to contribute and put information about you out on the Internet. Yet people still behave as if they are invisible on the Internet. People will post "funny" write-ups about themselves for the people in their social circles. Yet they do not realize that everything that is posted with their name on it can easily be associated with them. It's like the person who picks their nose while driving in their car down the road.   Sure it's a disgusting habit, but people do it in their car because they feel as if they have anonymity. They think no one is looking, never mind the fact, that all of their actions are on public display and people are looking.

Almost all news articles which cite stories of people being fired from stuff found on MySpace or Facebook contain the sentiment, "I didn't think anyone reads my blog" or "Why would people care what I have to say" or "It was just a joke". The fact is, that many people, including your employer, care what you have to say. Just ask Bob Namechanged. He was fired from a major big box store for integrity issues for writing the following on his MySpace page, "Drop a bomb on all the big box stores, trailer parks, ghettos, monster truck shows, and retarded fake 'pro wrestling' events, and the average I.Q. score would probably double."

Funny, maybe. Maybe not. It depends on whether or not you believe the stereotype that all people who shop at this particular big box store, live in the ghettos and trailer parks or attend truck shows have low I.Q. It was enough for his employer to feel like they could fire him for cause. After all, why would the big box store want to offend its customer base? Where Bob, and most people like him went wrong was making the joke in the first place. Secondly, in today's world, Bob made a mistake by assuming that he had the anonymity or the deniability he needed to make statements like that. Had Bob made the comment to a coworker in passing, it likely would not been enough to fire him since it would be Bob's word against his co-worker's word. Unfortunately for him, he recorded his comic thought on his MySpace page which was easily reproduced by the big box store. He failed to realize that when you associate yourself with a comment that can be reproduced it is difficult to argue against it.

There should be no doubt in your mind that your employer, people you work with, and people who know you are turning to the Internet to find information about you and those around you. Sure they might not tell you they've been snooping in your business. Societal norms prevent people from telling you that they have been poking around in your personal life, but rest assured you've been searched for more than once.   This prying leads us to a place where privacy and separation between all aspects of our lives no longer exist. Yet, the Internet provides information about you and those around you all of the time to people willing to look for it. And the sad part is, the skill level required to find this information decreases daily.   Furthermore, there are more things available to find as more content is published about you.   Better yet, the tools to find the information are being refined, and in most cases, improved.

Many people believe they can hide behind the protections offered by the websites they subscribe to. For example, many people will say that with the protections offered by sites like Facebook and MySpace, they are safe. And to some extent they are right.   They have the capability to lock their profile down to only the people they give access to see their profile. In theory, this lock down on their profile should protect people from the dangers of putting information out on the Internet but often it does not.

Yet, what happens when the people whom you have entrusted with the information found on your MySpace or Facebook page use that information against you? Let me tell you a little story about Darla Madeupname. Darla, was an employee of a grocery store chain in Canada.   Darla, along with 186 other people became a fan of a group on Facebook dedicated as a gathering place for current and past grocery chain store employees. When one of the group's fans, brought the postings of Darla to the attention of management of this grocery chain store, Darla was promptly fired. Never mind the fact that Darla had been given several raises and a promotion in the few years she had been with the company.

What Darla wrote online isn't important and neither is why the company fired her. What is important is Darla thought she had anonymity because someone couldn't find this information by using a search engine. In order to access this information a person has to subscribe to these groups. This often gives people a false sense of security. Unfortunately for Darla, the people she interacted with provided management with access to this private information. By interacting with people on the internet, Darla gave away the ability to remain anonymous.

It would be one thing if you were the only person who would put information about you on the Internet.   In that case, it might actually be possible to keep yourself anonymous on the Internet. However, you aren't the only player when it comes to keeping information about you off the Internet. People and organizations that are associated with you somehow, can write all about you and post it on their website at anytime.   Depending on what is put out about you on the Internet has the ability to help or harm you. With every new post on a blog or on a post on a Facebook or MySpace page, information about you on the Internet has the potential to grow.   The days of avoiding the Internet are rapidly decreasing.   You seemingly won't be able to hide.

WHY PEOPLE ARE SEARCHING FOR YOU?

Chances are you run into people you barely know all the time. So why not pry a little when you don't know someone very well? It sure is easy to find information if it is out on the web.   The ability to attain knowledge on your own has never been easier. We are able to find out the who, what, when, where, why and how of almost anything. The best and somewhat troubling part is it is getting easier to do so. While there can be a strong argument made about the reliability of the information which can be found on the Internet, it only matters which information people discern as credible.

Moreover, it has become common practice for people to re-search the unknown. When we travel to a new place, the information you need to make better decisions awaits you on the Internet.   Twenty years ago, the inability to find information usually gave an excuse for misdeeds such as going on a date with a psycho or not researching a company before a job interview.   Now, researching on the Internet is the expected practice before meeting with someone you don't know or going to a job interview.

This trend of easier access to information will continue to the point where finding the right information on the Internet is as second nature as breathing.   Back in 1995, search engines weren't very good at finding you the right information.   Crafty web site owners were able to manipulate search engine results and thus searching often resulted in crappy results with lots of links to porn sites.

Now, Google has rewritten the rules of the game for search en-gine technology.   With improved search technology, people are start-ing to get to the information they seek. Usually the difficulty resides in the user for providing too broad or too narrow search terms.   People search for each other for a multitude of reasons.   The term "Googling" has been coined to mean to search for someone or something.   (Ku-dos to Google for making themselves into a verb.) When you "google" someone you are attempting to find all of the available information about that person so you can make an informed judgment about them.

Some search out of curiosity, others search to protect themselves, some search to verify the truthfulness of what they're being told.

While the practice of "Googling" might be considered an invasion of privacy at worst and prying at best, it is becoming accepted as a societal norm. Someday real soon, it will be just what you do before and after you meet someone. Even if people won't admit to searching for information about you, because of the anonymity the Internet has, it doesn't have to be socially accepted. It can happen all the time and I'm here to tell you that it is happening right now and at increasing pace. You can thank the trends of the early 2000s for that.

SOMETHING HAS CHANGED SINCE 2003, ENTER WEB 2.0

Over the course of the last five years, we have seen explosive growth in the social aspect areas of the Internet. Socializing on the Internet exposes your private life in a public medium. Whether it's Facebook, your personal blog, or your children's blog, there are so many ways that you can be exposed on the Internet. But the damage doesn't stop there. As companies ask you to socialize on their websites by soliciting comments or content from you, you are contributing further to your online reputation. Better still, the companies use your comments to sell product, allowing those remarks to live forever (at least until they are no longer useful). You can do quite a bit of damage to your reputation long before you realize what you have done.

Don't blame the companies for the destruction of your online reputation. Those companies have a good reason for doing it. They want to make their websites more useful to you and other customers. The focus of many companies' efforts in the early part of the 21st century will be to make the Internet experience richer through user involvement. To facilitate the tools necessary for user involvement, enter the concept called Web 2.0. Web 2.0 is not an upgrade, per se to the Internet. Rather, Web 2.0 is a trend of what companies are trying to do to make their customers interact more with their website.

Companies aren't going to do you any favors when it comes to protecting your online image. Companies have realized that user involvement adds value to their Internet endeavors. The more people that use the user interactivity features, the higher the value for the company. In return, the company creates loyal customers by appearing to value the opinion of their customers. While most companies have seen the explosive success of the social networking sites on the Internet, they have learned the lesson and figured out how to take advantage of the social networking trend for regular websites. Companies now provide you with a way to interact on their website. If the company sells product, you can read and write reviews of products for sale on their websites. If the company writes articles, you can comment on those articles.

Web 2.0's focus is user involvement. The websites which are built for the sole purpose of user involvement are referred to as social networking websites. These companies center on photo sharing, video, networking, and blogging websites. Publishing to these media types, especially video, would have been almost next to impossible for an average user a few years back, now can be accomplished with the click of a button. Through innovation and the advent of new classes of product, the ability to publish video and photos has never been easier.

Social networking companies like Facebook, YouTube, and MySpace are driving people to publish content in droves. It works for the social networking companies because all they need to do is provide the tools with which people can interact with one another. It works for you because you get free space on some fun technology. It can be quite enjoyable to catch up with old friends, or make new ones which is why these technologies have really taken hold.

However, the tools the social networking companies provide would be worthless without you. In fact, the more outrageous things these companies can get you to do on their technology, the more value you add to their community. For instance, consider the case of Chris Crocker, and his "Leave Britney alone" video. While most of us agree that Britney Spears should be left alone, his video was a bit over the top in support of leaving Britney alone. We rushed in droves to view the videos and even the spoofs of the videos on YouTube. You can bet YouTube wasn't complaining about all the bandwidth his video was eating up on their servers. Not to say that these companies like it if you make a fool out of yourself, but they are not going to stop you.

Additionally, companies which provide services to you like social networking, want you to tell all about yourself. Now you might ask, well why would the company care about my interests and my demographic information? The answer is simple, money from targeted advertising. The better the company knows you, the better they are able to put ads in front of you which you will actually pay attention to. The better these companies can match up ads that people will look at, the better the company can get paid from advertisers. Think of how valuable knowing your romantic relationship status is to people who want to market a singles website. Now, what if they knew you were looking for a relationship. The advertisers would practically trip all over themselves to get an ad in front of you.

While providing the most private details of our lives might be fine for the companies' marketing efforts, the fact of the matter is they are not going to stop you from putting information on the Internet which could hurt you. Rather, they want anything and everything you will provide them. Unfortunately, when a person starts putting information like religion or sexual orientation out on the Internet it can impact their life. As was the case with a Las Vegas Catholic school teacher who was fired for posting he was gay on his MySpace page. In this case, it was enough to prove that he acted contrary to the beliefs of the Church which is why he was dismissed. For the Catholic school teacher, the Web 2.0 technology burned him badly.

The focus of web 2.0 technologies is to increase user involvement through collaboration with tools such as message boards, social networking, and blogs. The industry has signaled that it intends to provide the tools necessary to support the Web 2.0 demands of the Internet community as a whole. Further, the Internet community has welcomed Web 2.0 technologies with open arms. So I wouldn't hold my breath waiting for these technologies to go away.

ADAPTATION OF SOCIAL NETWORKING

The Internet generation, people born after 1975, has been very quick to adapt to using Web 2.0 technologies, like social networking. Seemingly, the younger you are the more likely you are to have a Facebook or MySpace account. In a study conducted by the Pew Internet & American Life Project towards the end of 2006, found that 55% of teens age 12-17 have created profiles online. But a closer look at the statistic shows the 15-17 age range had 64% of teens with profiles with 70% of teenage girls age 15-17 having profiles on social networking websites. But social networking is not just a teenage fad. Over 80% of MySpace users are over 18, and the fastest growing demographic of users is the 30-plus demographic. As a society we have embraced social networking with open arms. We have allowed ourselves to write about what is on our minds at any time with no regard to the impact on our online image.

Most of the recent press has demonized social networking because of the inherent risks involved. It is not that social networking websites are inherently evil. In fact, social networking sites are a good way for people to connect. Unfortunately, it is when people put up things that could hurt them in their future endeavors. In a study done by the University of Florida focusing on its 800 medical students and their use of Facebook, the University of Florida found about half of its (362) medical students had a Facebook page. Of those that had a Facebook account, only 37% (134) of the students, turned on the basic privacy feature which would block their profile from being publicly viewable. That means 228 future doctors had private information available publicly on the Internet. What they did find however, was how loose the would-be doctors (over 50%) were with their private information. The would-be doctors published their political opinions, sexual orientation, and drinking habits all over their public facing Facebook pages. I don't know about you, but I for one don't want to go to a doctor who is on the sauce when they are deciding if I am having a heart attack or a bad case of indigestion.

FALL OUT OF WEB 2.0

What we are starting to see are the ramifications of a very public, private life. To some segments of the population, this is nothing new. Celebrities have dealt with tabloids exposing the most intimate details of their private life for years. As such, celebrities have learned to avoid the spotlight and when they do have a problem, to involve someone who can do damage control. For the average John Q. Public, the consequences of exposing their private life on the Internet is starting to sink in. As firings over social networking, blogs, and websites increase, people are responding by pulling back on use of the available technology.

There are several high profile cases where people have been fired for blogging, but what we are seeing is the tip of a very large iceberg. Most employment discrimination that occurs because of what is published on the Internet goes unannounced. It happens before any interview ever takes place. Any organization, company, or person which has a selective process for candidate evaluation (employment, college admission, dating, etc.) is going to use the Internet to assist in the decision making process. People are going to soon learn that their misdeeds of the past are going to cost them dearly when they attempt to reach their goals unless they change their approach to the Internet.

To date, most of the discussion in the Online Image Management community has been about prevention and/or recovery of unfavorable content. So in effect, people are attempting to become anonymous by removing themselves from the Internet through prevention and recovery methods.

The focus on keeping yourself anonymous, as best as possible, is misguided. In a world where all of us can be researched on the Internet, not having a presence can be worse than remaining anonymous. Over the course of time, the societal expectation will be that you can get a good feel for who someone is by viewing who they are online. If you can't view information about that individual, the assumption will be that you are a nobody, you have no professional connections, or you have provided a false identity. It will be difficult for you to succeed in an increasingly smaller world. Even if you were to successfully hide, which I know is somewhat doubtful; it probably wouldn't be the best course of action for you. It's quickly becoming a catch-22 for many people wishing to remain anonymous and wanting to be part of society. However it doesn't have to be.

SUMMING IT ALL UP

People are using the Internet to find out about anything and anyone. Don't blame people for causing you this headache, chances are you've done it too. What you need to be asking yourself is, "how am I going to react and adapt to this new reality?" The focus of how to use the Internet from the individual perspective needs to shift from seeing the Internet as your enemy to using the Internet as a tool to help you separate yourself from the pack, in a good way. Controlling how you appear on the Internet will help you reach the goals you desire.   As time marches on, it will not be optional to control how you appear on the Internet, it will be expected.

Embracing the Internet and effectively portraying yourself on the Internet for the world to see will be the critical social skill of the 21st century.

CHAPTER TWO

WHO YOU ARE ONLINE: YOUR ONLINE IMAGE

"Character is like a tree and reputation like a shadow. The shadow is what we think of it, the tree is the real thing"

—Abraham Lincoln, American President

The Internet is being used as a tool to determine who you are in real life. While what you can find on the Internet is definitely lacking when it comes to being able to determine who a person is, it doesn't matter. People *think* they can find out about you using the Internet. To be able to control how you appear on the Internet, you need to understand how people see you. From here on out, let's refer to what people can find about you on the Internet as your online image.

It will be helpful in understanding your online image to draw parallels with your real life. In real life, how you present yourself to other people tells a lot about you. The appearance of your clothing; your personality; your posture; your friends; your humor; your vehicle; and your spouse reveal details about who you are. These attributes contribute to who you are from an outside point of view. Based on these attributes, someone can speculate about education level, wealth, status, and power among others. Because society places so much value on these items in determining who someone is, people tend to naturally practice image protection in their real life.

PRACTICING IMAGE CONTROL

To control how people perceive us, we practice image control. Corporations, politicians, and celebrities are very well versed in image control. They recognize the value of perception and why they need to control that information. Like politicians, we seek to control what types of information is shown to certain types of people. We try to manipulate our image as if we control an image prism. Depending on how we hold the prism, the picture they see changes. The prism then shows them what we want them to see. If we were to take who you really are and put you behind this prism, some people would see aspects of you and others would not. The prism effect provides different views as to who you are based on the audience and their past history. For instance, if you want to show yourself to a prospective employer, you would show an image of yourself as the dedicated employee. What you choose to reveal about yourself defines an image of who you are.

So understanding your online image is rather simple. It is how you want to be seen when someone searches for information about you on the Internet. OK, so that's fairly straight forward. Now, what constitutes an online image is where the concept gets more interesting. An online image consists of the information that can be found and perceived as you on the Internet. Notice the words "can be found" and "perceived" in that sentence. Not all information that exists about you on the Internet can be easily found. Further, information which might look like you, will be attributed to you. It doesn't matter that the information isn't yours. If it looks like you, it will be attributed to you.

All of the information that can be found shapes an image of who you are, an online image. If you are like most people, you probably didn't realize what your online image is. But nonetheless, because you didn't know what your online image is or know that it exists doesn't mean that people don't see it every day in one shape or another. Your friends see your image when they search for you. Past lovers see your image when they are checking up on you. Friends of your friends see your online image when they are looking at your friends. Prospective employers see your online image when you are going for that awesome job which allows you to work from home and get paid for web surfing. Complete strangers see it when they are searching for things that have nothing to do with you, but your online image ended up in their search results. In the end, everyone sees who you are online, anytime and anywhere, and for whatever reason they sought you out.

AN OCEAN OF INFORMATION

It would be a mistake to think that your image is the total combination of all the information about you on the Internet. A vast ocean of information exists on the Internet. Some of the information out there is about you but the vast majority of it is not. The ability for that information to be found depends on how well that information is connected with other repositories of information. What you need to be concerned with is the ability to make the pages that you don't like disappear and the ones that you do like come to the top of the pile.

Like in real life, your online image is not a complete representation of who you are, but merely what people can learn about you. An online image is how you appear to the online world. What we chose to reveal about ourselves can greatly influence our online image. If you reveal your hobbies, you tell people that you are someone who cares deeply about that hobby.   For instance, let's say you do quite a bit of posting on model railroad websites.   This would indicate to people that you are passionate about model railroading.

The information available about you online is a patchwork of text /images/video spread across the multitudes of websites. These tidbits of information are online, scattered about and would be difficult or even impossible to find without use of search engines (e.g., Google, Bing, and Yahoo!)

As people adapt to using the Internet to perform duties they used to have to take extreme effort to do in person, your online image is going to be much more vital to your life.   How someone uses this information is what determines if your image is positive or negative. And to make matters worse, you aren't in complete control of your image.   Your online image is available to anyone who cares to view it at any time, in any Internet capable location.

YOUR ONLINE IMAGE: AN ONLINE PICASSO

Have you ever seen a Picasso painting? If you have, you know two people can look at a Picasso painting and see completely different things. Your online image is an online Picasso, completely up to the interpretation of the person seeing it, to make sense of who you are. Multiple aspects of your online image are shaped by varying players. For instance, your online image is shaped by the search engine results. If you perform a search with the key words with your name on Google and on Yahoo, you will find a different result set for each of the two search engines.   Each of the results give different pieces of the puzzle that is your online image. They only see parts of who you are and make assumptions based on stereotyping to fill in the rest.

Further complicating the issue is the location of where the information is found. In other words, on which website did the comments attributed to you show up. To illustrate this point, let's assume that you are a Human Resource specialist and were researching the job applicants for a particular job on the search engine, Google. If you were searching and found a product review on Amazon, you might not think much of it. Now if the same product was offered for sale on a sexually oriented website and the exact same comment was made on the exact same product, you would associate the reputation of the website it was found on to the person who made the comment. The same conduct applies in our normal lives. For example, if you take the above scenario and apply it to your normal life it would be as if you were seen in your real life going to the supermarket and buying size D batteries, most people would think nothing of it and realize you had a legitimate need for size D batteries. Now, if someone sees you walk into a sexually oriented store and walk out with size D batteries, all of the sudden their mind goes places it never should and you are now known to them as a sexual deviant. Like a Picasso, it depends on the context in which you view the information.

Your online image is quickly becoming your professional image. Elements of your online image will make or break you in the years to come. Like generations before, you manage how you present yourself at work, job interviews, etc. For example, you know to wear work appropriate attire and how to interact with your coworkers. If you fail to maintain your professional image by dressing inappropriately or not acting like a team player, you can damage your image at work. Nothing hurts promotion opportunities like a damaged image. Now that employers are turning to the Internet to research you, your professional image is what they can see online.

However, you have more facets to your online image other than your professional image. How you present yourself at home, with your friends, and with potential dates are all image contributors to your online image . For example, if you write about your love life online, your love life is now part of your online image. Your online image takes all of these facets of your image, like a Picasso, and synthesizes them into one image. Your online image is a multifaceted picture of who you are to the worldwide audience.

WHEN YOUR WORLDS COLLIDE

In order to understand how to present yourself on the Internet, you need to realize how you currently present yourself in your real life. We are all masters of presenting ourselves whether or not we realize that we do it. As social creatures, we learn cues from others on how to appropriately present ourselves to each other. Presenting ourselves appropriately is something that we innately do with varying degrees of success based on our level of social intelligence. Our social intelligence dictates to us how to present ourselves differently to people depending on the context of the situation and to whom we are interacting with. The degree to which we are successful in presenting an appropriate image of ourselves depends on how high our social intelligence has evolved. If our social intelligence is low, we might have difficulty understanding the nuances of social interaction. If your social intelligence was low, you probably wouldn't care who you were online. So feel good about yourself, you probably have high social intelligence.

In your real life, you are able to maintain multiple images of yourself that select people see. At work, you show your professional side. You know, the side of you that punctually shows up early and energetic. The side that is always willing to go the extra mile for the office and look for new ways to do your job better. It's that side of you that keeps getting praise for your hard work. You are able to manage who you are at work and most of your coworkers probably don't know what you do when you drive away from the office.

Once you get away from the office, off goes the professional image and you become another side of you. Let's call this the afterhours you. Maybe the afterhours you head bangs to 80s music as you speed out of the work parking lot. Once you get home, the afterhours you plops down on the couch for some Seinfeld reruns. After a couple hours of that maybe you get ready to go out for a drink-till-you-make-a-fool -out-of-yourself party. (Or maybe you like to cross dress. Maybe you attend a toastmasters meeting. Who cares you're off the clock.)

Every so often, you need to pay a visit to your Grandma and this is when you become the Grandma you. The ultra sweet, anything you say, yes ma'am, I'm serious about getting married, you. Grandma would expect nothing less and you definitely want to present your best image towards Grandma. One thing is certain, you definitely do not want Grandma hearing about your binge drinking.

THE 1980s' WORLD VERSES TODAY

Before the Internet was in widespread use, let's call it the 1980s' world. In the 1980s' world when the multiple sides of you would come into contact, manageable disasters would potentially occur. For example, maybe one of your friends knows somebody who knows your boss at work. Through this birds-of-a-feather network, your boss hears what you really think of the pathetic, bumbling, not qualified for the job, person he/she really is. In the 1980s' world, you had the ability to react, defend, deny, and destroy. Sure this nightmarish scenario of boss truth telling could happen from time to time and you may or may not have lost your job. Although terrible and certainly not desirable, most of what your boss had heard was hearsay. In other words, the evidence was a based on rumor. The great thing was you had some options to defend yourself. You could deny the rumor altogether, you could downplay the rumor, you could explain your comments, you could discredit the rumor by painting the source as a power hungry snake, or the new boyfriend of your ex, intent on making you lose your job.

Compared to the 1980s' world, today's interconnected world is a veritable hell when it comes to image management. In the brave new world of the Internet, it's much harder to discredit or deny rumor if there is evidence of the transgression. Your professional and private life which you worked hard to maintain separation, collide in unanticipated ways. In the 1980s' world, if people wanted to destroy your reputation, they had an agenda. Now, people who are merely taking advantage of the technology, can destroy your reputation with a few clicks of the mouse.

The Internet, combined with the age of digital media, has made it difficult for people to maintain their privacy. What you do late at night can be as easily pinned on you as what you do during the day. What's worse, is everyone can see it across the globe. What's even worse than that, you don't know how to even begin defending your reputation. People who barely know you can find out enough information to disqualify you from a job, deny entrance to college, refuse to date you, so much for those late night drink-till-you-pass-out-while-cross-dressing parties.

The different shades of who you are at work, at home, and after hours tend to come into contact in the online world. Your parents might be building a family blog website and end up posting that out on the Internet. Meanwhile, your employer may need to promote you because you are a hit conservative talk show host for their radio station. At the same time, your friends are blogging about your wild and crazy exploits on the town last night. When this happens, the contradictions between your personal life and professional life can impact your career.

Even people who are pure as the driven snow can be subject to an invasion of privacy which they don't deserve. If you are posting your efforts on your latest interview on your blog, it's a bit awkward when your employer asks you how your job search is going. Additionally, it's fairly uncomfortable when your mom asks you when you are going to introduce your boyfriend to your parents when your mom has read all about your visit to his parents house two months ago on your boyfriend's blog.

STEREOTYPING MAKES YOUR ONLINE IMAGE WHAT IT IS

So what's a stereotype have to do with your online image? Absolutely everything! Stereotypes are the mechanism by which we make decisions about people on the Internet. We do this because the Internet really is limited in what information it can provide about a person. Forming quick opinions is what we do best. If you subscribe to Darwinism school of thought, we have been bred to do so. It's in our nature. And frankly the world is too big and too complicated to make sense of it without them. Let me illustrate this point this way, if we go back 6,000 years or so, (if you don't subscribe to Darwinism), people were living in a kill or be killed sort of world. In order to make it to the next day, you needed to decide quickly if you were dealing with a friendly creature. The people who could make the decisions quicker lasted longer and made more babies than those who could not make quick decisions. Thus the traits for making quick decisions were bred into us over time.

The necessity for making quick decisions is the foundation for the use of stereotypes. A stereotype allows us to summarize a situation, a person, or a threat. These stereotypes simplify the information gathering process which helps us react. When we encounter limited information on the Internet, we look for clues so we can apply a stereotype that fits the information we are finding.

We all are familiar with stereotypes and use them daily. Using stereotypes to communicate in our daily lives helps information transfer faster. If someone were to tell you about a guy and the description they give you is, "He's a nerd". Automatically, your mind draws for you the stereotypical beanpole, complete with acne, braces, and pocket protector who is into some technical sort of field. Right or wrong, this stereotype conveys the information you need to make a judgment call on whether or not you want to deal with them.

Want more proof of the use of stereotypes in our daily lives? Much of our humor depends on stereotype. Common jokes such as blond jokes depend on the perpetuation of the dumb blond stereotype. While unfair to people with blond hair, these stereotypes are perpetuated because people tend to look for these qualities when interacting with people that fit the mold of the stereotype.

Unfortunately, when people make up their mind that a stereotype is true, they tend to find the supporting evidence they need to confirm their bias. They notice when the "woman driver" in front of the cut them off, or when the "fatty" is gorging themselves with hot dogs and chili cheese fries. As a parent, we label our kids teenagers so we have some explanation for the behavior they exhibit from time to time.

What's worse is people will often people will try to perpetuate the stereotype themselves if they think it applies to them. If they have been characterized as a teenager, they will rely on the stereotype from time to time to use it as an excuse for their behavior. If they are known as a jock, they will try to party and avoid schoolwork, in order to maintain the image.

However, we all use and need stereotypes because we are often in situations with limited information. If you consider all the situations you have faced throughout the day, you will soon realize how often you characterize something based on past experience or cultural stereotype. There is simply too much information to process without them. If you had to understand everything about a situation in order to make a decision, you would not be able to make the decisions you need to in time. Without stereotypes, being able to make sense of the online world would be quite difficult.

Stereotypes take quite a bit of flak, because of negative cultural use of stereotyping. The whole discipline of political correctness exists to counter negative stereotyping. The problem with stereotyping is when we apply negative stereotypes to people. Negative stereotypes that characterize people based on race, religion, gender, sexual orientation, political stance, are generally too limiting to make correct judgments and always unfair to the person, especially if the information is found online.

Humans are much too difficult to really know over a medium like the Internet, but that doesn't stop us from trying. In real life, getting to know someone is difficult enough.   After ten years, I still learn things about my wife that I didn't know. (I expect to learn even more over the next 50 to 60 years.) The Internet can provide you with pictures, text, movies and sound, but it will never give you the capability to interact as humans need to do so we can get to know one another. You can't exchange a glance, you can't read body language as easily as you can in real life. You can't judge how someone acts and reacts in certain social situations. When you think about it, interacting on the Internet will never be a substitute for real life interaction.

We can all agree that online information is much too vague to say who a person is. It is not right to judge someone unfairly without regard for truth based on little evidence and the appearance that they fit the mold. If you have ever been on the receiving end of a negative stereotype you know exactly how unfair those stereotypes are. But reality is reality, people use online information to stereotype all the time.

IN THE EYE OF THE BEHOLDER

The process of making decisions is often automatic and depends greatly on what experiences we have had in our lives, the culture we live in, and the stereotype biases we have. In order to illustrate how a person uses the Internet to make quick decisions, let's take the case of someone applying for a position for a small company. First of all, Judy, the hiring manager, must screen all of the candidates. At this point in time, Judy has just been given the stack of completed applications which includes your application. Judy makes her way through the stack of applicants and creates a pile of people to review further. Fortunately for you, you're still in the running because you meet the basic qualifications and hey, your resume is impressive.

Before we proceed too much further, let's make the assumption there is information about you and your close inner circle of family and friends on the Internet. This information may include pictures, resumes, stories, personal genealogy, group affiliation, and so on. This information is scattered all over the Internet and not lumped together in one definitive resource.

Like most managers, Judy typically forms opinions of who she is going to hire long before the first interview, based on what she has seen to that point. Besides presentation of the resume and job history, Judy uses the Internet because it provides a great anonymous resource to find out the things a candidate doesn't tell in a job interview or application. Being curious, Judy wants to find out what else she can discover about a particular candidate. And who can blame her, the Internet is the best resource the world has to offer, for this sort of sleuthing.

Judy heads off to her favorite search engine. Because Judy knows that a likely way to find results about you is to search for your name as it appears on your resume. Once the search results are returned, she will start sifting through the myriad of search results to determine who you are in your real life. This kind of searching will be hit and miss. Some results will belong to you. Other results will belong to people who share the same name. Many results will probably have nothing to do with you because of the current state of search engine technology. Whether or not these results get attributed to you depends highly on the interpretation of the searcher. Some web pages will probably be easy to say, "OK, that's right he lives in Bakersfield, CA." This type of information is credible and factual and thus it backs up what's on your resume. It makes them feel like you've been honest so far.

Other types of information found will allow for interpretation. For example, from this picture Judy can tell that you look like someone who is fun to party with. Maybe that's accurate and maybe it's not, it doesn't matter. This information typically leaves it up to Judy to apply her very own interpretation of the information found.

Now Judy, being moderately crafty, decides to search based on some of the other information she has at her disposal. Judy decides that the e-mail address is a great piece of information to use as a search term. The results Judy finds from this sort of searching will be immediately credible in her mind because your e-mail address is unique. All of the sudden, a wealth of information is at Judy's disposal because you actively participate in newsgroups and message boards which require your e-mail address.

Judy now can go and assess if you are the type of person that she wants working for her company. (Hopefully, those sexist jokes about women managers you posted 10 years ago aren't included in the search results.) At this point, Judy needs to start making decisions about who you are and whether or not she should bother with an interview. Satisfied that she has you figured out, as the sexist pig you are, Judy moves your application to the circular file.

All of this information in its entirety, gave Judy an idea of who you are. Whether or not the idea of who you are is accurate (I believe you! You are not the sexist pig the Internet says you are.), the information that is available shapes Judy's opinion of you. Unfortunately, all of the pieces Judy found helped her make a decision not to interview you.

This idea of who you are has been formed in Judy's mind and is quite negative. Keep in mind, Judy had never met you, doesn't associate with people that know you, and yet, she feels like she made the right decision. Judy made up her opinion about you based partly on past experiences she has had in her life. Using her point of view of the world and those in it, Judy applied her life lessons and stereotype bias to figure you out.

Using the information she has gained from the Internet, Judy uses her set of stereotypes to classify who you are in her mind. In this case you were a sexist. Being labeled as a sexist was completely detrimental to your chances for employment with the company. Being labeled as sexist was unfair to you as well. But that's not what is important. What is important and what you need to understand is how Judy came to her conclusion.

STEREOTYPE BIAS

Judy used her set of stereotypes to make the decision about you. Judy carries with her thousands of stereotypes all given to her by her family, friends, and culture. She uses her stereotype set to make sense of the world and for the most part she is unaware of her bias. Her stereotype set is huge when you consider the thousands of stereotypes we share.

Thousand of stereotypes might sound excessive until you consider all of the words that carry stereotype meaning. (Let's try going A to Z for fun. American, blond, conservative, druggie, emo, fatty, girly girl, ho, Irish ,jock, kook, lawyer, Mormon, nerd, oppressor, politician, queer, racist, socialist, teenager, urbanite , womanizer, xenophobe, yuppie, zealot.) Furthermore, stereotypes cover the spectrum of all aspects of life. In this short list, a broad range of topics ranging from political leanings, national origin, religious beliefs, gender bias, personality, sexual orientation, sexual promiscuity, and age bias. So when applying stereotypes to your online image, there are plenty to choose from. The goal will be to control the stereotype you are portraying.

Judy displayed stereotype bias in labeling you as a sexist. While she doesn't know for certain you are a sexist, you seem to fit her idea of one. Her failing to recognize that she is applying stereotype bias is unfortunate and something she needs to work on. Unfortunately, it does you no good when you are standing in line waiting to apply for unemployment.

Judy's stereotype set is influenced by her culture. In large part, this is done to maintain culture. Cultures tend to perpetuate stereotypes to frame outsiders as different. For example, in the United States there is a negative stereotype of a Mexican. In Mexico, native Mexicans don't have a negative stereotype of themselves; rather they have a negative stereotype of a Gringo. Furthermore, cultures tend to use stereotypes as a mechanism for maintaining social control. Fear of having a negative stereotype applied to her can keep Judy from acting in certain manners. Fear of being stereotyped as a racist will keep her from using racial stereotypes in public. If Judy were reviewing the resume of someone who was Hispanic, Judy would be certain to not let stereotype bias show in her decision if she has such a bias, yet it still may come through. Thus, stereotype bias is often difficult to detect even when it is being applied because people like Judy don't realize they are being biased.

So, as in the case of Judy, the stereotypical stereotyping hiring manager, we saw what stereotypes do when they work against our desires. The point however, is not to convince you to avoid the use of stereotypes, but rather understand that your online image is completely shaped by stereotype. It is very important that you learn about stereotypes and distinguish between positive and negative stereotypes so you can use them when you manage your online image. Using stereotype to your advantage online is vital to managing your online image successfully.

The nature of the Internet, with rather limited information about a person naturally leads us to stereotyping the information we find out about people. Knowledge and application of positive, applicable stereotypes will make all the difference when someone is trying to figure out who you are online. The goal should be to control the message so you can help form a positive first impression and a positive stereotype.

THINGS THAT CLOUD THE PICTURE OF WHO YOU ARE ONLINE

In order to accurately portray who you are online, it is important to address areas that can obscure your online image.   If left alone, these image modifying bits of information can cause people to get the wrong idea about you. If there is a lack of information about you on the Internet, people can assume a few things about you. For starters, if on your resume, you claim to be a leader in your career field, you should have websites that support your leadership roles. Lack of information in this case, leads someone to assume that you have falsely stated your leadership role which is one of the last things you would want.

Furthermore, lack of information available about you, gives more weight to the information that is available. For instance, if the only information out on the Internet about you is a quote you gave to a student newspaper in college. "I think work is for losers. Anybody that wants to work 9-5 is a joke. Down with the man!" Immediately tells the person looking at this tidbit a few things. Primarily, they can see you have authority issues, and secondarily they can tell you don't like working hard. Never mind the fact that you were joking around when you gave the quote and you were trying to impress a girl. The problem is the information lacks the context of the situation. Unfortunately, these bits of information can be all it takes to eliminate you from the high paying job.

Poorly written comments that are directly identifiable as written by you can misrepresent your intelligence and writing capabilities. When found by people, these types of information can be telling about the amount of time you spend writing, how in depth your thinking process is, how well you can defend an argument, how well you can articulate your points of view.   You surely don't want someone making a judgment about you based on a comment you posted on a website at 2 A.M. while watching SpongeBob.

Anytime you write something that will be used on the Internet regardless of the website, take the time to do it right or post it anonymously.   If your comments are well written and insightful, this can demonstrate that you are a consummate, intelligent individual. (Guidelines for writing web content and comments will be presented later in the book.) Further complicating the process is the fact that people share your name across the globe. Information that belongs to them could be mistaken as yours.   It's a classic case of mistaken identity.   Chances are, your namesake on the Internet is not going to bolster someone's opinion of you.

In the case of mistaken identity, if it is positive information, it might work to your advantage. However, if the information found is a video of your namesake making a jackass out of themselves for the entire world to see, then perhaps it is time to make certain that the people you know will be searching for you are directed where you want them to go, rather than having them haphazardly stumble about the Internet and using the first tidbit of information about someone who shares the same name as you.

SUMMING IT ALL UP

Your online image is much more important than any of your other real life images (professional, at home, and after hours) because those images are limited to those people who come into contact with you and your associates. Damage to your real life image is contained because it takes someone who knows you to spread the damage. Additionally, most of the people you care about realize there are multiple sides to a story when hearing rumor or gossip. Your online image doesn't have to have someone who knows you to spread the dirt. The dirt is available at anytime, anywhere and is accessible by everyone. An online image will be the cornerstone to most of your social interaction. If any of the real life images become damaged they are effectively walled off from the other images. Your online image transcends and influences all of your real life images.

Understanding the stereotypes that shape and form your online image will be vital to effectively controlling your online image. Knowing the stereotype that you want to portray will be how you effectively manage what people think about you. Not making the effort to shape the stereotype leaves it up to everyone else to form the stereotype of who you are.

Your online image will be the key to surviving the 21st century. Any damage to your online image will impact you socially and economically. As such, your image needs to be safeguarded as your most valuable asset.

CHAPTER THREE

WHY YOU SHOULD MANAGE YOUR ONLINE IMAGE

"We all live in a televised goldfish bowl."

—*Eleanor Roosevelt, First Lady*

As you have learned, the trends of the Internet in the early 21st century have involved user interaction.   Increasingly, we are all turning to the Internet to fulfill aspects of our need for social companionship. From looking up past classmates to socializing on Facebook, everywhere we turn the Internet is becoming the tool for social interaction. Embracing the Internet and effectively putting yourself out on the Internet for the world to see will be the critical social skill of the 21st century.

The boom for social interaction on the Internet began with the Internet generation. The Internet generation, those born after 1975, use the Internet as the ultimate social tool.   What makes this generation unlike others is the unabashed use of technology. This generation appears to not care about the potential impact of what they have posted online. They are actively creating information on the Internet with no thought of keeping information private. This generation uses the Internet to profile other people. They use the Internet to make friends and set up dates and black ball each other. They are making MySpace and Facebook gobs and gobs of money. Since the Internet generation owns tomorrow, they are defining the rules for the 21st century. As such, this generation is the group that is propelling the Internet into the ultimate social resource network.

So why go to the effort to manage your online image? The simple answer is because I said so. What? That's not good enough for you? You need something more concrete to make the leap of faith into Online Image Management. OK then, let's break down why you should manage your online image.

WHO NEEDS TO MANAGE THEIR ONLINE IMAGE

Early in life we are taught the importance of image and why people are popular or not by our peers. As we are segregated into groups of popular and not, we learn of the benefits of being popular: you get to tease rather than be teased, get to go to more parties, have more friends, and set the trends. Popular kids present themselves in ways that popular people behave. If a person gets the unpopular label, they are quickly cast aside to fend for themselves. Shunned by the popular group, unpopular kids take solace in chess club and a box of Twinkies.

From these early life lessons in image management we learn that our peers initially view us as they see us, not as we are. Our peer's opinions of us are shaped by our friends, our clothing, and little things like the rumor mill. As a result, we learn to modify our image to meet expectations of those around us. At first, we attempt to make people to see us as we want them to see us even if that is not who we are. Only after trust is gained, do we let down our natural defenses and let people in.

The same rules from childhood also exist into adulthood. The main addition to the childhood rules is there are more labels to apply to people. No longer are the labels limited to unpopular, popular, fat, skinny, pretty, smelly, and/or ugly. Now, as much more mature adults we can apply labels according to characteristics of individuals such as personality, profession, success, race, religion, gender, and sex to name a few. In our efforts to avoid a derogatory stereotype, we attempt to manage our image in our adult life so we can be seen as a positive stereotype. In general, we attempt to take our life lessons and apply them to any situation.

As in childhood, when we lack information we turn to whoever we can to help us find the information we need. Whether it be parents, siblings, teachers, friends, or imaginary friends, we utilize the resources we have available to us to find what we are looking for. As 21st century adult, we have learned to turn to the Internet when we can't find information about someone so we can make the call on if they are worth our time.

With the Internet being the ultimate rumor mill complete with rumors, speculation, facts, and much, much, more about you, is it that far of a stretch that one should expect that people will turn to the Internet to find information about someone they don't know? Further, does it take a great leap of faith to believe that it might be important to most aspects of your life to protect yourself from people getting the wrong idea about you? If you are with me on these premises then you should protect yourself as best as you can. The best way to do protect yourself on the Internet is to not ignore what information about you is on the Internet.

Professionals such as doctors, dentists, and lawyers already realize that their professional reputation impacts their bottom line. Consider what could happen to a plastic surgeon's practice if someone alleged malpractice and told their friends. The surgeon might lose business depending on how egregious the allegation was and how many friends the patient has. Now consider what would happen to a plastic surgeon's practice if someone were to make a video showing a patient's botched face-lift on YouTube. Malpractice lawsuits aside, if the botched face-lift is even slightly botched who really wants to go to that surgeon? If the face-lift is hideous, the surgeon's practice doesn't have a prayer of surviving without a major advertising campaign. As such, professionals who depend on their reputation as a service provider, need to protect and manage their online image as they protect their professional practice.

Is Online Image Management just for those professionals who could lose their livelihood? Hardly! Online Image Management is for everyone. Online Image Management is for anyone who ever had anything to lose by having a damaged reputation. Online Image Management is for anyone who has ever had to compete with other people for a job. Online Image Management is for parents who need to keep their children from making mistakes that could hurt them when they try to get into college or start their careers. Online Image Management is for anybody interested in dating someone they just met. Online Image Management is for anyone who deals with the public. I could go on, but I think it suffices to say, Online Image Management is for everyone! Yes, I realize there might be someone out there in the Amazon who has never heard of the Internet let alone a computer. But, for the rest of us who aren't isolated from the world and have to participate in it, we need to be managing our online image.

THE APPROACHES YOU CAN TAKE

You have a choice as to how you manage your online image. You can be reactive or you can be proactive. Either choice carries with it consequences. If you choose to be reactive you can let your online image be and do nothing while others post things about you with no rebuttal from you. Only when it gets to be a problem would you get involved with Online Image Management. However, if you choose to be proactive you can be an early adopter and start managing your image now to get a leg up on the competition.   Hopefully, you will choose to start managing your online image.

BEING REACTIVE AND DOING NOTHING

If you still are not convinced that you should act, think again. The anything goes approach may work with the free love environment of the 1960s, but will not work with your online image. With an online image, meddling is the only way to have the Internet present you the way you would like to be presented. Otherwise, you're at the whim of everyone else on the Internet to say who you are.

If you really consider it, would you rather people got their information about you from you or that they got their information about you on a website put up by your past significant other. Most people who are concerned with the way the Internet portrays them for the most part, have been taking a hands off approach. They believe that by publishing nothing they are protected from the Internet. After all, if they aren't publishing content about themselves, how on earth would they get in trouble for information out on the Internet? Empirical evidence has taught them throughout their lives is the best way to deal with something which can be a nuisance is to not associate with it. So far they think they have been very successful at managing to keep personal information about themselves from unauthorized access on the Internet.

Unfortunately, the motivating factor for these people to stay away from the Internet is fear. People are concerned for good reason. The impact from all sorts of scams and identity theft can be horrendous. Having your financial identity stolen can be quite difficult to recover from. Furthermore, it can get quite expensive to restore your good name. However, creation of an online image will have little to do with whether or not these fears are realized. There are so many other non Internet ways someone can get at your identity or learn about you. The Internet just happens to get all the publicity.

In reality, most cases of identity theft don't occur because you used a credit card on a shady website. Rather, the hospital, company, and/or government agency you entrusted with your social security number, personal information, and credit cards were not exercising their fiduciary responsibility in protecting your information. In essence, identity theft occurs because you trusted someone with your *private* information and they lost it.

Over the years now and again, I have received letters in the mail notifying me this or that credit card number has been compromised. But recently, I was a victim of identity theft. The hospital, which lost my social security number and health information, informed me in writing of the loss and offered to pay for a year's worth of credit monitoring. (A nice gesture.) When I looked into it further, it was interesting to see where the information was lost. The hospital had done their part to make sure my information was protected. My information was lost in transit between the company and the offsite backup storage facility. The eighteen year veteran courier for the backup storage company failed to follow protocol which was to take the tape backups immediately to the backup storage facilities. Rather, the courier left the tape backups containing 1.7 million individual records in the back of their car. As Murphy's Law would predict, someone smashed the window of the car in the middle of the night and walked away with tape backups. There are no suspects to date and the local police department offered a $1,000 reward. (Yet another nice gesture) Was the loss of my personal information a result of me posting information on the Internet? No, of course not. It was out of my hands at that point After all, what could I have done differently?

Would managing my online image prevent the loss of my data? No. But it wasn't the cause of the data loss either. The cause of the data loss was misplaced trust. I trusted someone (the hospital), who trusted someone (the tape backup storage facility) who trusted someone (the courier) who trusted that someone (the thief) wouldn't steal it in the middle of the night. Internet aside, as the loss of my data illustrates, you simply can't avoid the consequences of a computer based, data driven, connected world.

It is not possible to keep yourself off the Internet and it would not be wise to do so. There are multiple fallacies with this approach. For starters, not having a presence doesn't mean you don't have an image. Having nothing on the Internet about you doesn't give you anonymity. It means that to the seeker of your information, you are unimportant. Either you don't exist in their world or you're not up to date. It says in a booming voice, "no one cares enough about you to publish information about you".

Economically speaking, the world is getting smaller because more people across the globe are competing for the same resources you are. Geographically, the boundaries that once existed in business dealings are gone. For instance, you can do business with someone in Moscow as easily as someone in your local neighboring community.

Professionally, it can portray that you don't participate or contribute in your field. Professionals who lead in their industry tend to show up in online discussions. You can see traces of their image on book reviews and comments made on news articles that they have an educated opinion on.

Furthermore, it's naïve to think that you are the only person who could put damaging information about you on the Internet. If you are social and the people within your circle are Internet publishers it should be safe to assume there might be something of consequence on the Internet. With the advent of digital cameras, there are too many ways to get pictures of you on the Internet.

Unless you have kept yourself off the Internet altogether, you probably have things you've written scattered all over the Internet. Past e-mails, comments, and guestbook signing are just a few ways things can just magically show up on the Internet. All of these can be used to make assumptions.

By not participating in the technology, you'll likely to be left behind. With newer generations now actively embracing the Internet like no generation before, it won't take long before it is expected to know the ins and outs of these technologies. Your only viable solution is to embrace the Internet as if it were an old friend.

BEING PROACTIVE

Embracing the Internet means that you adapt to the reality of the Internet. It doesn't mean that you should go out immediately and start buying I heart Internet T-shirts. However, it does mean that you realize that our online world is here to stay. With that realization, you recognize that the Internet is a part of everyday life and growing in its importance in decision making.

Because of the apparent tidal wave of Internet capable devices and appliances, we should be more prepared to accept the fact that traditional privacy is fading and will soon be gone.   Gone are the days when you were known only to members of your local community. The Internet is now a source for rumor mill and speculation.

The effort involved to manage your online image will be substantial. After all, it is going to take bit of work to set up everything you need. The choice will be yours, of course, you will need to consider everything you have to gain by managing your online image.   More importantly, you will need to consider everything you have to lose by not managing your online image. Using tools like WhooRu.com can make it easier to manage your online reputation. Every day more and more tools are being made available to help you manage who you are online.

GETTING AHEAD OF THE GAME

The world is a pretty competitive place. In this shrinking world, you will need to compete for most things that are of any worth. Companies compete with each other for profits and customers. With companies, often the competition is so intense, companies are willing to take losses on certain items to draw you into their store and not the competitor's store. Those companies that fail to recognize the need to compete often lag their competitors in terms of profits, innovation, and customers. Once the company becomes complacent, they lose their competitive edge. With people, it's not much different. There are only so many resources in this world to go around. We all compete for financial resources. For each job that exists, there are several people willing to take it. And like companies, not all of us are clued in to the competition. Those who fail to compete lose out to competitors for employment, dates, college admission, scholarships, and so on.

In order to compete for shrinking resources you need to create advantages. Normal advantages for individuals include attaining the appropriate education and experience for your chosen career field. Your online image can enhance your advantages and make you competitive, thus creating a competitive advantage. A competitive advantage means that you have something advantageous that others do not. Armed with a competitive advantage you will get more of the opportunities you seek than if you had no competitive advantage. Without a competitive advantage you're just another resume in the pile.

In the case of Online Image Management, the competitive advantage you will enjoy is employers will get a better feel for who you are. This will help employers determine whether or not you are a fit for the position they are trying to fill. Additionally, other people will not be using the same techniques you do, so competitively speaking, they are at a disadvantage. If you maintain your image over the long run, you will be able to enjoy a sustainable competitive advantage because you will be ahead of others in this field and already figuring out the next best way to use the Internet to advance you and your agenda, long before the competition.

How far ahead of the competition would you be if you choose to practice Online Image Management? In a 2007 Pew Internet survey of adult Internet users, the majority 60% of adult Internet users don't even care what information is available about them on the Internet. Those of the 40% that do care, do very little about it. The most they do is monitor the Internet for personal information. The reason for this is that the Internet is still quite mysterious to many of us who don't speak geek. (Those that speak geek aren't socially intelligent enough to realize that their success in the social world depends on the Internet. There I go perpetuating a stereotype).

The best thing that could happen to you would be for Online Image Management to never catch on. In that case, Online Image Management would make you something special in the eyes of the beholder. It would be as if you were in the land of the blind and you were the person with one eye. Your sustainable competitive advantage would propel you into greater opportunities. Whether those opportunities are better schools or better dates, the only thing that matters is they are opportunities you wouldn't have had otherwise. But let's face it, pretty soon it's going to be hard to compete if you don't manage your online image. I fully expect Online Image Management to be vitally important in the coming years.

EMPLOYERS AND THE INTERNET

With so much at stake, it's important to focus on some of the most important areas where an online image can help you the most, employment. Unless you are born into wealth, employment is important because it's the difference between living in a home and living in a van down by the river. Within the labor market, the better you can compete, the better type of job you will be able to secure. When money is at stake, you owe it to the people who depend on you for their daily bread to do your part. And doing your part includes managing your professional image so that you can compete.

You've been competing in a global labor market for some time now, you just didn't know it. The Internet has removed the geographical boundaries of where and how a business can conduct itself. For example, the practice of off shoring to low wage economies has exploded in United States in the past ten years. The Internet, lower wages, and a skilled job force in India have made it possible to move call centers, IT infrastructure, and software development from the

United States. IT professionals in the United States now compete for the same jobs with similar professionals around the globe. This trend of off shoring will continue as long as businesses can cut costs while maintaining acceptable service levels.

I know your shedding big salty tears for those overpaid IT computer guys, but consider this: no job is safe from being impacted by the Internet. Those of you, who think your job can't be outsourced because your job requires you to physically be there in person, think again. McDonald's has shifted its drive through order operators from Hawaii to Texas in an effort to make its workers at the fast food restaurant more effective.   Order takers in Texas are trained to use local colloquialisms such as "Aloha". (How's that for the personal touch. Let's hope they avoid the phrase "y'all come again, ya hear".) The ability for someone in Texas to interact with someone in the drive through lane in Hawaii is made possible only with connectivity from the Internet.

While potentially frightening to all drive through order takers, the good news is the jobs haven't been eliminated from the market. The jobs have just relocated. Companies will still need to fill the jobs that have moved. Hopefully, your community has been able to land a few of them. The current landscape of the environment for employers is going to drive employers to take talent wherever they can find it. In the near future, the baby boom retirement will be in full swing. Talented individuals with vast experience will be leaving the labor force right and left. This will mean that companies will be facing a shortage of skilled labor the likes of which they never have seen. The competition between companies is going to be high for the talent they can find. With the talent being harder to find within local markets, employers will turn to the Internet. Companies will have to scour the Internet to search for talent. Having your online image out there properly promoting you will draw these employers to you.

The people who are going to fill many of these jobs are going to be the Internet generation. The Internet generation is going to have computer skills that tomorrow's companies are going to need to compete. Furthermore, they are not afraid to try new things. After all, the Internet generation is constantly bombarded with new technologies to learn. The Internet generation will be more connected with trends in the industry because they have embraced the Internet. For those employees outside the Internet generation, they will have to make themselves relevant through Online Image Management just to keep up.

With there being such a premium on talent, employers will need to turn to the Internet find talent but also to minimize mistakes. The Internet helps employers find out anything they can about a candidate to avoid a costly mistake. One bad hire can be disastrous for the morale of a company as well as costly in terms of lost productivity, training expense, and hiring expenses. With these costs, employers can't afford to make many mistakes in the hiring process.

Employment opportunities most of the time are going to go to the candidate who appears to be the best fit for the position. With the Internet as a tool, employers feel as if they can make better decisions because of the ability to ascertain the character of an individual from a few web pages. After all, the last thing an employer wants is a sexual harassment lawsuit waiting to happen if they hire someone with those kind of comments out on the Internet.

To be competitive, multinational companies will need to take talent wherever they can find it. This means, companies are going to be looking for talent across the globe in places such as Singapore, London, New York, Bangladesh, or Pocatello(Idaho, USA). As a result, you will be evaluated across cultural and geophysical boundaries with candidates in every corner of the earth. Your salary will not be determined by your local or national economy, but what you are worth on a global scale. This type of competition means you are going to have to compete with people of comparable skill who have much lower salary demands than you.

Companies welcome the new realities facing the workforce because it lowers their overall costs while increasing and diversifying their talent pool. But does it work for you? In a sense, it does. The more opportunity available to you is fantastic. You will be able to compete in markets when your home market is undergoing a recession. You will have access to multiple companies with vast opportunities for advancement. Where it doesn't work for you is how are you going to compete with someone who will work for a fraction of what you would be able to? The answer is to convince the company you are worth every penny that your "bargain" salary demands. In order to convince them you are going to have to deliver a more effective message than your resume. Everyone has a resume, but not everyone has an online image that works for them. Your command of the Internet, shown by building an online image, will be a mechanism you use to persuade them to show you the money.

To persuade a prospective employer, you are going to have to show that you are special. With Online Image Management, you can go into more depth than a resume can provide a prospective employer. The possibilities are endless once you have an employer checking out your online image. For starters, a great way to show off experience is to give a detailed case study on projects that you have been involved with. For instance, you can make it easier for employers to understand your role in saving the company a million dollars annually. Once you can provide evidence of how you fit in with your current employer, it will make it easier for them to see how you will work within their company. Additionally, you can provide evidence that you are active in your field. By posting on appropriate career field related sites, you can show your expertise. By reviewing books appropriate to your field and blogging about professional activities is yet another great way to show your skills.

With so much at stake when it comes to employment, how can you afford not to manage your online image? The world is shrinking and you will need to find your niche inside it. With Online Image Management, you will have the tools you need to properly present yourself in a manner appropriate of a professional in your field.

IMPACT ON YOUR LIFE OUTSIDE EMPLOYMENT

I focus on employment because of its ability to impact you in the pocketbook. However, I don't wish to minimize the impact in other areas of your life. Certainly employment is very important, but it's not everything. Your online image has a massive impact outside of employment. From dating to college admission, your online image impacts everything.

Back when I was dating my future wife, (which was when the Internet was going through the dot com craziness) I had a personal website. It was a typical website for someone in college. I had an about me section, with quite a bit of self admiration. I had information about my family complete with pictures and tell all stories about them. Of course, I had a friend section. In particular, I had a friend, Mandy, who happened to be a close friend of mine. She and I had gone through high school as good friends -- nothing more, nothing less. I wrote a bit about Mandy on my webpage in which I stated she was special to me, as a friend. My girlfriend, wanting to give her parents some insight about me, directed her parents to my website. To my chagrin, I ended up having to explain to my girlfriend's mother that there was nothing going on between Mandy and I. Ultimately, no damage was done. But the lesson was learned. What I had on my personal website almost cost me my sweetheart.

Countless other stories are out there about googling a potential date. Could you blame someone for checking out someone's online image? In an age where the dangers of a blind date almost exceed the value of such an encounter, it seems a blind dater needs to protect themselves. In fact, I recommend to anyone that they find someone's online image before dating. Its analog comparison would be asking friends of a friend if they know anything about their date. There are definitely burned ex's who have posted documentaries on their ex's philandering. College buddies who post their buddies' nickname "lipwhore" out there. Let's pretend for a moment, you are the one who has all of those things out on the Internet. Of course, none of this makes you a bad person, just maybe not dating material.   The reason why people check other people out online is risk reduction. We have all heard stories about the nightmare blind date. If you could find something that might keep you off that nightmare date, wouldn't it be worth it?

Sitting on the other side of the fence is the person hoping to go out on a date with them. Online Image Management can help them appear to be safe and not the "lipwhore" reputation they earned in junior high. They should try to ensure that the Internet doesn't portray them in a bad light. After all, isn't Mr. or Mrs. Right at stake here?

ONLINE IMAGE MANAGEMENT VS. IDENTITY THEFT

A common misconception about Online Image Management is it is identity theft protection. Often, people will confuse Online Image Management with protecting their social security numbers and financial information.   Identity theft is a serious problem. The danger of losing personal information gives someone the ability to apply and receive credit cards, and work under your good name.   The practice of protection of those juicy tidbits of information is known as identity theft management. Because of the pervasiveness of identity theft, people think that what we are trying to do is synonymous with identity management.   In reality, identity theft management is only loosely connected with Online Image Management.   The focus of identity theft management is to keep identity fraud or other types of crime from being perpetrated on you. Identity theft management attempts to protect you by limiting the loss of personal and financial information such as Social Security numbers, credit card numbers, and bank accounts.

Most of us, fortunately, are smart enough not to post this type of information on the Internet. However, it doesn't take a lot of information to steal your identity. The information needed to apply for a credit card is quite minimal.   A would be thief needs only your full name, your social security number, your date of birth, your mailing address, your employer, your title, and your pay rate.

It's true, there are a couple pieces of information in that list that aren't readily available of the Internet already: Your social security number and pay rate. But, the pay rate can be made up based on an educated guess on what your position pays. Whereas, the social security number, might be difficult to make up. All of the other data, can be found with a few websites (e.g., http://www.birthdatabase.com, http://www.pipl.com) or with other means. Means such as dumpster diving, copying your information from corporate computers, or stealing your mail or wallet.

Putting an online image on the Internet doesn't put you at more risk for identity theft. The approach Online Image Management takes is to make certain you only put public information out on the Internet. Blaming the Internet for identity theft is like blaming the water pipes for carrying water to your home. The Internet is only the means of transmission. It's what website owners are doing with the information they collect via their website which leads to identity theft. The Internet gets a bad rap because companies have made it possible to apply for financial instruments like credit cards and loans without ever meeting you. The ease of which someone can apply is like adding gasoline to a fire. However, other means are much more effective at identity theft than scouring the Internet for people whose identity would be good to steal.

With identity theft management, you are attempting to thwart the efforts of would be financial identity impostors by restricting and avoiding the use of those personal tidbits. While identity theft management is very important in a digital age, it is rather short sighted in its approach. The focus is elimination of any of the information that could harm you financially.   Yet, identity theft management doesn't speak to the information which can help you.

Often, people who attempt to eliminate as much personal information about themselves on the Internet, make every effort possible to remain as anonymous as possible. They will monitor their credit report.   They will actively seek out any information that appears to be damning about themselves and ask it to be removed.   Often, if a company that they transact business with asks for a social security number, they will refuse to supply it and go somewhere else.

In contrast to identity theft management, Online Image Management is holistic in nature. Identity theft focuses on a narrow segment of information, while Online Image Management, broadens its reach by seeking to control all information about you on the Internet. Furthermore, Online Image Management is focused on the proper presentation of your digital self. With Online Image Management, your digital reputation is very important to maintain and provide information which will be useful to individuals who do not know you.   With Online Image Management, you are trying to put the right types of information about you on the Internet while limiting access to the wrong types of information.   In actuality, publishing information about yourself might actually help counter an identity theft attempt. By creating a highly credible resource about you on the Internet, you can put a face with your stolen information out there for people to see.

Also if someone is looking to steal your identity, they may consider the prominence of the information about you on the Internet as a good reason not to steal your identity.   They know, like you do, that sooner or later someone is going to go searching for your stolen name on the Internet.   If they are using your identity for employment purposes, it will eventually backfire on them.

SUMMING IT ALL UP

If you fail to manage your online reputation, you will suffer the consequences of not doing so.   Basically, every aspect of your life which is controlled by a person making decisions about you is at stake. Your current job, future jobs, enrollment in selective schools, business dealings, loans, and legal defenses are just a few of the aspects of your life where the Internet can impact you. If you want a particular job or to go to a selective university you might have troubles doing so if you have a dirty online image.

Online Image Management helps you control how you appear on the Internet. Using the techniques described in this book, you should be able to tame your information currently on the internet and add only the information you believe to be appropriate for your online image.

CHAPTER FOUR

THE IMPACT
OF YOUR SOCIAL NETWORK

"Associate with men of good quality if you esteem your own reputation; for it is better to be alone than in bad company."

—*George Washington, American President*

Have you ever gone to the movies to watch a comedy in a packed movie theater and noticed that when people are laughing, you laugh harder? We are social creatures and as such, our lives are enriched by the people we associate with. We share laughs with our friends. We tell scary stories around a campfire with our kids. We go to church to worship together. We all desire to belong to a group. As such, we crave and seek out ways to find one another. Our lives revolve around our social contacts. From our holidays to our friendships, our need for social interaction draws us together, rather than forcing us to live isolated lives in the middle of the wilderness.

From our home lives to our workplace, we have connections between each other which creates our social network. These connections help us with all aspects of our lives, from emotional support to job hunting. We access our social network on a daily basis.

Our individual social networks intermingle to create even larger networks. We are all interconnected and most of us seek to draw more connections between us all. We seek out these connections through development of friends and associates to make our network stronger. The stronger our social network is, the stronger our capacity to accomplish the goals which require a social network such as finding love and providing for our families.

The largest social network that exists on this planet can be referred to as the global social network. In the global social network, every person you know has a connection to you.   Every person you know has connections to people they know, and so on. The connections that bind us together are the glue of the global social network. One might think traversing the global social network can be difficult. However, research in the field of social networking shows, globally, we are within six contacts of any person on the globe.   That means, in a world of 6 billion people, the mere fact that you and I are connected by six people or less is simply amazing.

This concept is known as the small world phenomenon or also known as the six degrees of separation. In popular culture, this is often referred to as the "Six degrees of Kevin Bacon". The concept was that anyone could be tied to the American actor, Kevin Bacon within six contacts or hops on the network. Being a good sport about this, Kevin Bacon starred in a Visa check card commercial where he wants to write a check to buy the book "Guitar Picks", but the clerk states, "I just need to see some ID". Kevin states "hold that thought". Kevin leaves the store to track down people so he can tie himself to the clerk. Upon returning Kevin states, "Okay. So I was in a movie with an extra, Eunice, whose hairdresser, Wayne, attended Sunday school with Father O'Neill, who plays racquetball with Dr. Sanjay, who recently removed the appendix of Kim, who dumped you sophomore year. So you see, we're practically brothers." You should check out the video on YouTube. It's definitely worth a look.

One important distinction to note is the global social network has always existed regardless of technological advancement. Back when there were only a few thousand humans inhabiting the planet there was a global network. Hundreds of years from now, the global social network could become the interstellar social network. What technology has done for us, in terms of the global network, is to have enhanced the ability for people to see your interaction within the global network.

With the advent of the Internet, people have tried to make the Internet work to achieve the same needs they have always sought out. The early Internet provided some ways for us to reach out, connect, and express ourselves. Before the social networking sites, people sought out chat rooms to connect with other people. Some people made their websites using free website companies, other people looked for love on the Internet. All the while, companies started creating the tools necessary for us to connect more efficiently.

Although still in their infancy, the tools of social connectivity are now becoming prevalent in our society. The companies who make these products want to capitalize on the basic human drive to connect. What's more, these companies are going to continue making products which will drive us further into socializing over the Internet. One thing for certain, as time marches on, the Internet and our technology will continue to further fulfill the human desire for connection.

As social networking tools become more prevalent, the ability for anyone to track your social network will become much easier. When we and/or the people around us use social networking tools, we leave digital footprints all over the web. These footprints leave evidence our activity on the Internet. The footprints are in a traceable format made easy to find by search engines. Perhaps you are thinking to yourself, "I don't need to worry. I wouldn't know what a Facebook was if it jumped up and bit me in the butt. I certainly don't have anything out on social networking websites". Even if you do not know how to get on a computer, your social network can be exposed by people you know and even people you don't. Talk to some of your family members and see if they have posted any pictures of you on their Facebook or MySpace account. I think you'll be surprised. You'll see pictures of you that you didn't even know existed.

What should matter most to you in this ever growing global network is how you are perceived on the network. On the global social network, you reputation is your most valuable asset. It is vitally important to control the first impression of you because it's all about managing what people think who don't know you. It is the difference between having a full time job and waiting in the unemployment line. In order to successfully manage your online image, you need to be equipped with the skills to identify, conceive, build, monitor, and defend your image.

MAKING THE CONNECTION

Our once imperceptible social networks are becoming more visible as time marches on. With the advent of social networking sites and blogging, our ability to see the lines of connectivity between people are becoming clear. We are able to draw the connections between your friends and their friends' friends and their friends' friends and so on. You may have lost that job opportunity because somehow, someone connected you to BillyBob the self described catfish hunter who likes to fish with dynamite. What makes the online world so much more potentially damning is the fact that for the first time, people with very limited means can track down and map your social network.

Online, our personal social network is quite a bit easier to discover than in person. For comparisons sake, in the 1980's world, if someone had wanted to find out information about you and those whom you associate with, they would have had to know someone within your immediate social network. Now, with the Internet, the connections between you and your social network can be determined with a little cyber sleuthing. With very little effort, someone can map all of the sites/people that associate with you.

What's even better, is we are making it easier every day to help establish visible social links. We, ourselves, are drawing the lines for people to connect us. With social networking sites such as Facebook and MySpace, we connect ourselves to our close associates. While these sites are fun, different, and a good way to socialize, it may be difficult to explain away blog postings about the "fill in the blank" you did in high school. Furthermore, do you really want pictures of you on the toilet posted by your friend. If you don't think that is possible, try searching for "Taking a dump" on youtube.com.

Not all is lost. Just because someone can see who you are connected to isn't a bad thing. If you control your visible connections, your social network can be one of the most influential aspects of your online image.   Identification of what your network is and isn't can help you manipulate and control it so that you are able to present yourself in the best possible light on the Internet.

YOUR SOCIAL NETWORK

Ultimately, your online image on the web is created by you and those around you. In real life your image is directly impacted by people you associate with and whom they associate with. We have sayings that teach us this lesson such as , "Tell me who your friends are and I will tell you who you are" and "Birds of a feather, flock together." As you have probably already witnessed in your life, making the right contacts will help you. Making the wrong contacts, will make things worse. It's not important whether or not you believe this to be true, many people subscribe to this way of thinking. So identification of people who are easily associated with you and possibly publishing on the Internet matters quite a bit.

In terms of your social network, you are the center of the universe. The world, so to speak, revolves around you. (I know you're thinking, "Finally somebody gets it"). For most, it would seem that their network consists of close family and friends. However, you have circles of people that you interact with on the global social network.

Outer Circle

Social Horizon

Middle Circle

People that are highly likely
to write or post pictures about you

Inner Circle

Past Relationships, Friends and Family
People who call you by your first name
Close Business Relationships
Groups you are
actively participating in

acquaintances
people who know people in your primary circle
people you recognize and they recognize you
Groups you affiliate with

People you don't know
People that dont know anyone in your primary circle

There are three main distinctions of people you interact within your portion of the global social network. Closest to you is an inner circle of people who are nearest to you on the network. You also have a middle circle of acquaintances, and an outer circle consisting of everyone else in the global social network.

It is through the inner and middle circles that you are connected to the outer circle which makes up the rest of the global social network. Your contacts within these two circles help you interact with the global social network. The broader your inner and middle circles are, the more capable you are in interacting within the global social network. All of your life you've probably heard this concept explained as, "it's not what you know, it's who you know". Without these groups, you would be isolated, penniless, and unattractive. (OK, the unattractive part might not be true.)

For the purposes of managing your online image, you need to identify who is in your inner and middle circles. Everyone, including you, Mr. or Ms. Center of the Universe, has skeletons in their closet. People with potential access to these skeletons need to be identified and monitored (not destroyed). This identification of the circles is very important because you will be able to apply the appropriate level of monitoring.

Information that could be harmful to you might be present on the Internet thanks to people within your inner and middle circles. This information posted by your inner and middle circles, is what people in the outer circle, (which is beyond your social horizon), use to determine who you are.

THE INNER CIRCLE

The people around you, whom you have the most interaction with, make up the inner circle of your social network. If you prefer, you can think of this as "the circle of trust". This circle would include our family, close friends, current and past romantic interests, and/or close coworkers whom you know on an informal basis. Essentially, these are the people would know you the best and would be able to describe who you are in greater detail than anyone beyond this circle. These people live and play around you. Your inner circle cares about you and would likely be the group that shows up at your funeral.   A good rule of thumb to identify if a person is in your inner circle is whether or not you interact with them in your free time.

Your family should be an obvious choice for inclusion within your inner circle. When it comes to family, inclusion in this circle does not depend on the closeness of the relationship. If society places a stereotype on the relationship that would imply closeness, then you need to consider that person part of the inner circle. For instance, if society believes that a mother should be close to her son, comments made by her would carry more weight if they were to be published by her than say a regular Joe Blow off the street. It simply does not matter how close you are to a relative if they decide to post pictures about you on the Internet. People on the global social network will make the assumption that you should be close and attribute the family member's comments accordingly.

Current and past romantic interests should be included within your inner circle because they too, would be likely to write about you. These types of relationships in particular need to be watched because their emotions will allow them to set aside normal societal norms and post whatever they are feeling at the moment. For example, if you had wronged a past lover, they may write pretty lousy and unfair things about you on their blog. Worst yet, if you one day become famous, they might be willing to sell that video you made late at night in the privacy of your home.   You know what video I'm talking about. If not, just ask Paris Hilton. Simply put, these past and current relationships demand closeness and as such would be capable of disastrous results to your online image.

Other people within this circle would include the groups that you interact with. Perhaps because you love hunting you attend National Rifle Association (NRA) meetings on a frequent basis . Maybe you attend People for the Ethical Treatment of Animals (PETA) meetings after the NRA meetings are over because you care about all of the orphaned animals. After that, you attend an Emotions Anonymous (EA) meeting to help deal with the emotional conflict over your love of hunting and strong desire to protect animal rights. Groups like these have websites and sometimes will post news releases and membership rosters without your knowledge.

While membership in these groups is fine for whoever wants to belong to them, it is the stereotype associated with the group that carries weight. Knowledge of what these groups will do with your information is important in protecting your online reputation and why they need to be included within your inner circle.

The people within your inner circle would be the group most likely to want to write about their interactions with you on the web. This fact alone makes the group the primary circle of focus. Their unbeknownst to you postings can be some of the more damning information posted about you.

THE MIDDLE CIRCLE

As we move away from the center of the universe (you), the potential for damaging information working its way on to the Internet goes down. The middle circle of your social network would be the group of people that you know on a formal basis or as an acquaintance. You might not even know them personally, but someone within your inner circle does. A good rule of thumb for inclusion within this circle would be that you could recognize who they were or be able to draw the connection to you with one or two people between you. However, there is still potential in the middle circle for information to get out about you and it's worth paying attention to it. While you may only know people on a formal basis, they may just want to be associated with you. It doesn't matter their motives, all it matters is they know of you and could potentially post about you.

Additionally, inside the middle circle would be the group of people that interact with people on your inner circle. We usually refer to these people as friends of a friend. Since we are all individuals, we all have our own social networks. Your father has a social network complete with people that he tells stories about you. For instance, people within your Dad's inner circle could know detailed stories about you even though you would consider those people to be acquaintances at best. Nevertheless, people in this group are worthy of middle circle status.

The middle circle would also include membership in groups that you no longer participate in, or participate in as a passive member. The reasons for monitoring these groups would be the same as monitoring groups you actively participate in. You simply may not want to be counted amongst their ranks. While not as potentially damaging as the inner circle, the middle circle has potential to wreak havoc on your online image and should be monitored. Because of the middle circle's size, identification of this group will be more difficult than monitoring the inner group. The best approach to monitoring this group is to identify and monitor people who seem to like attention and spreading gossip.

THE SOCIAL HORIZON

If you have ever witnessed a sunset, you have witnessed the sun dipping below the horizon of the earth. In social networks, there is a point at which you cannot see what is beyond the social horizon. The social horizon is the transition between the middle circle and outer circle. Your social horizon is also the social boundary where you cease to have acquaintances and connections to your inner circle. Both of these groups, the inner circle and the middle circle, are within your social horizon.

THE OUTER CIRCLE

As we move to the cold areas of space away from the center of the universe (you) we start to encounter strange beings. These are people whom you don't know and have no easily traceable connection to you. This group of people is known as the outer circle. The outer circle would be those people who are beyond your social horizon.

If you found information posted about you on the Internet from a member in the outer circle, you would probably be scratching your head for awhile trying to draw the connection between the website and yourself. What will be important in determining if their comments have validity is if people will associate the comments with you.

Why this circle is worth mentioning is because this is where most of the people who will make snap judgments about you without considering any other source come from. These are the people whom your efforts to influence and direct their attention to your online image will have the most impact.

SUMMING IT ALL UP

Globally, we are all within six people of each other. However, most people, (except Kevin Bacon,) can not draw the connection past a few people. So in order to learn details about someone whom you are not in direct contact with, you need to tap in to their social network. Once you open their social network, you can expand those who you can get your message to.

In Online Image Management, your social network is very important because your social network has the ability to shape your online image. Your social network knows you better than people who are outside your social network. Watching those key individuals within your social network will be key to protecting your online image.

PART II

WHAT YOU CAN DO ABOUT IT!

CHAPTER FIVE

INTRODUCTION TO
ONLINE IMAGE MANAGEMENT

"A reputation for a thousand years may depend upon the conduct of a single moment."

—Ernest Bramah, English Author

Most people are somewhat oblivious as to how the Internet has changed the rules of the game.   In the early days of the Internet, people were caught up with the dot com craze of the 90's.   And now they are caught up with the social networking of web 2.0.   While the trends are fun to get involved with, people fail to recognize how the Internet hurts them. Some people, however, recognize the true importance of the Internet as a medium for social interaction.   Fortunately, you are now one of them.

Now that you've had a chance to understand the importance of controlling your online image, you are probably wondering how on earth you're going to do that.   Up until this point, this book has been about the what's and the why's of Online Image Management. Now, we will turn our attention towards the how's of Online Image Management.

PURPOSE OF IMAGE MANAGEMENT

To address the challenges of image management in the 21st century, a new approach has to be implemented.   Gone are the days of doing nothing and hoping for the best.   Gone are the days of watching what shows up on the Internet about you with childlike bewilderment. It's time to take how you appear on the Internet into your own hands.

With Online Image Management, you are addressing the challenges of presenting yourself via an online image.   You will be creating an online presence, in most cases starting from scratch.   Controlling your online image requires you to invest yourself into the process. There is a bit of work to do up front before you start to reap the benefits as is the case of anything worth doing.   You will be researching your image, writing content, and promoting yourself to name a few of the activities of Online Image Management.   However, I suspect you will find the process enjoyable and worthwhile.

Online Image Management requires a holistic approach to tackle your online image.   By holistic, I certainly don't mean for you to start breaking out herbs, acupuncture needles, and shunning western medicine to build your online image. I simply mean that you treat Online Image Management as a complete solution of analyzing, building, protecting, and destroying elements of a bad image rather than focusing on just eliminating the symptoms of a bad image.   The holistic approach of Online Image Management is broad and encompasses all aspects about how you appear on the Internet.   There are many areas where your online image resides and unlike real life, where your image is a by-product of who you are and who you interact with, an online image is something that without proper care and feeding can soon get out of hand. From the creation of your image to the removal of bad elements of your image, your online image needs to be cultivated to the point that it serves you rather than harms you.

Essentially, with Online Image Management, you are trying to communicate with people. For this communication to occur there needs to be a message for people to receive. This message will be what you will create as a result of the process outlined in this book. To have an image you need to produce content which conveys the message you want the receiver to receive. In this case, you will craft the message to be transmitted via the Internet.

Your receiver will be the people who are expected to receive the message. We will call this class of people the target audience. You will have to make assumptions about your target audience such as do they look online for job candidates and do they have a high degree of sophistication. Distinguishing who exactly is your target audience is going to be essential. Is the target audience a future employer or your current employer? Perhaps the target audience is past friends and family.

The proper identification of the target audience will tell you which stereotype you need to try to have people associate with you. As we have learned up to this point, it's really in the eyes of the beholder, the target audience. The target audience member is going to apply their knowledge of how the Internet works and their stereotype of what someone like you should be. Armed with the knowledge gained in this book along with your social intelligence, you should have no problem creating the appropriate stereotype.

Ultimately, the purpose of Online Image Management is to make the Internet work for you. Embracing the Internet by placing your image out for the entire world to see shows that you are a not afraid of tacking on the number one social challenge of the 21st century. Having the Internet as your ally is the way to protect your interests. By changing your image from something that could get you fired into something that effectively communicates the right message, we are transforming your image into something that may get you that great new promotion or that new job at that cutting edge company.

GOAL OF ONLINE IMAGE MANAGEMENT

The key goal of Online Image Management is to effectively communicate who you are. In order to do so, we need to focus on the establishment, credibility, exposure and protection of your online image. We are trying to establish a credible, pleasing image of who you are at the same time giving your image the exposure it needs in order to be found on the Internet by Internet users with less than average skill. We take it one step further by protecting the image you have created by eliminating the information that does not suit your purposes. All of the efforts in this book will be to promote the goal of Online Image Management.

To accomplish the goal, the approach of Online Image Management is to control the message that can be found about you on the Internet. Perhaps it goes without saying, but to control your image you will need something to actually control. You will need to create the message by placing information on the Internet that reflects who you want to be in real life.

ESTABLISHMENT OF YOUR ONLINE IMAGE

All things worth doing take time and effort. If it were easy to do, everyone would have an appropriate online image. Yet, you get the online image you deserve. If you are unwilling to do the work, then you deserve to be cast off into the Internet wilderness. (Unless of course you are willing to pay someone to do it for you, in which case, welcome back to the land of Online Image Management.;)) SHAME-LESS PLUG ALERT: WhooRu.com for all your Online Image Management needs.

The initial challenge of Online Image Management is to determine what should be on the Internet about you. To establish your image we need the right information on the Internet about you. The right information is loosely defined as information that supports what you want your image to be. So it would follow, that information that does not support your image would be the wrong information to place on the Internet.

To determine your message, you will go through the identification phase as well as the conception phase. The identification phase will serve to identify who you are currently on the Internet. While the conception phase will go through the process of determining who you want to be. These phases will be outlined in greater detail later in this chapter as well as in their respective chapters.

One of the challenges will be figuring out who you are in real life. For some, this step will be easy because they have good self awareness. For others, it will be difficult because they are not sure of themselves and the direction they want to head in life. This might take more time for you to figure out who you are and where you want to be. But hey, you probably need to do it anyway.

Eventually, you will need to determine what you want to be seen as. First, you will need to create the message you want received. This step will be about introspection. You will need to figure out what you want to be and which stereotype to promote. Additionally, you will need to figure out what is currently out in the Internet wilderness. This way you will be able to tame it.

Once you know what your current image is, you will have to deal with your online image as it currently exists. Chances are your online image to date is most likely a hodgepodge of information posted by yourself, your family, and your friends. This online image will probably be detrimental to your task of effectively communicating. You may already have things on the Internet that you do not want to appear when people search for you. Furthermore, the information that is out there is not coordinated. While some information may be putting you in a positive light, other information may be contradictory. The contradictions will weaken your image and leave the target audience confused.

Further still, this information lacks the scrutiny which you will need to apply before posting on the web. As an example, there may be information from your blog. At best, the postings which can be found on your blog probably aren't oriented towards a targeted audience. At worst, you are mentally dumping into your blog. Mentally dumping is the process by which you write about whatever is on your mind at the time. Could be politics, religion, friends, or whatever happened to be at the front of your mind enough to dump it out. All of the information that is out there needs to either be dealt with accordingly or absorbed into your new online image.

Next, you will need to place your message on the Internet. It reminds me of the old adage, "if a tree falls in the forest, does it make a sound?" Well, if a tree is never planted, it doesn't matter if it falls because it never existed. In other words, you need to put your message out for the world to see.

We need the digital equivalent of you on the Internet. The best way to create your digital self is to have a single resource that is immediately identifiable as a resource dedicated to you and your pursuits. This single resource will be your own website. Your website will be the intended primary point of contact for your image. It will be the home for the most information that can be found about you on the Internet. You will put the majority of your effort into making certain that your website is current and updated. After all, if it looks like your website hasn't been maintained it weakens the effect of an online image.

In addition to the creation of your website, you will need to establish the message on multiple sites. While your website is a good way to create a home for your message, limiting yourself to that solitary resource would be misguided. First of all, your website will show up in the top 10 of search results, but nothing else you control would. By planting the message all over the Internet you strengthen the effect of your message. Second of all, your credibility is greatly enhanced by multiple sources of your image. We will use whatever resource is available to you to put your message on. Social networking websites, comment boards, professional blogs, news sites, industry specific message boards, and online product vendors like Amazon are just a few of the resources we will attempt to place your message. In the end, your message will be loud and clear for the intended recipient. By placing yourself out there and in front, there will be no mistaking who you are online.

CRAFTING CREDIBILITY

The Internet suffers from a massive credibility issue. The ironic part is that the source of the problem is the very thing that makes the Internet what it is: Everyone can create and publish web content. All of this content varies depending on the quality of authors which generate the massive quantity of information that can be found on the Internet. Websites suffer from credibility issues for a variety of reasons such as poor design, the authors themselves, bad location, scam risk, stolen content, poor editing, and the nature of the topic.

To counter the problem of the Internet credibility, online image managers need to be very concerned with the ways that content credibility can be established and destroyed. A primary way online image managers can destroy or establish credibility will be with the care they give to make certain that their material gives the appearance of credibility.

Almost immediately, the first impression of a website can do more for the credibility than almost anything else. First impressions are everything when it comes to stereotype and a bad design starts you on the path towards a bad stereotype. It just says so many dreadful things about you to have a poor site design. If the design is poor to start with, this signals to the end user that the company/person they are dealing with doesn't care enough to be taken seriously, or they don't know what they are doing. Perhaps, it states that you simply don't care. For instance, content that is riddled with grammatical errors display a lack of care and/or education from the author and does a great deal of damage to the credibility of the website. While content that appears to be well designed and organized shows the attention to detail that gives people the feeling they are dealing with a believable source of information.

The quality of websites varies as much as the people who produce them do. The ease of which content can be created by these authors causes poor content to proliferate throughout the Internet. These authors can sign up on websites and become authors/journalists without review from publishers or peers. Unfortunately, the lack of review also leads to low quality content being spread like noxious weeds on the Internet.

Your online image will depend upon the creation of a web of credible information placed strategically across the Internet. The goal of this strategically placed information is to validate the main source of your online image, which is your personal website. It is important to take advantage of existing websites which solicit user publishing and or commenting. You will be able to piggyback on their investment of time and money to build their reputation as a credible source. By adding content which can validate your published information on credible websites, you will strengthen your online image. When you marry your website with information that supports your image on the Internet, you create a highly credible resource you desire. Without purposefully placing information on the Internet, you are at the whim of what is available on the Internet.

People assign credibility based on the website where the content is found. In North American society, news sites have credibility because our society believes that news companies have journalistic integrity. This integrity drives these companies to validate sources, and print retractions if they ever find out something to be false. Other societies do not place the same distinction on the credibility of news organizations. However, because of these cultural biases, in the US, people give extra credibility to articles appearing in news organization's sites and publications. For example, people will give more credibility to a resource if it is an article on cnn.com verses an article written on Joe's blog on everything.

The credibility issue the Internet suffers from isn't helped by the increasing frequency of targeted scams. In the course of a single day, people receive several scams and illegal solicitations just in their e-mail alone. The potential to be burned by these scams and misleading information makes most people question the very nature of any content they encounter over the Internet. Thus, when people encounter a website, like yours, which is completely unfamiliar, people question the credibility as if by second nature.

To make matters worse, the credibility of the Internet content often, suffers from the author themselves. A prime reason websites suffer is because the author is not knowledgeable on the topic they are writing about. When an author misuses the jargon associated with the topic they are writing about, knowledgeable people of the topic will quickly discount the information. Additionally, this lack of expertise shows through in the writing style of the author. Dead giveaways are when an author stumbles through providing a technical description or when the author injects unrelated topics.

Further adding to credibility issues, several authors will plagiarize in order to build their website quickly. Most authors don't believe they will be detected. However, the plagiarism is quickly determined when search engine results come back and multiple sources have the same exact content.

Many of these Internet authors use their Internet space to write about whatever is on their mind at the time.   While this kind of mental dumping is interesting and fun to read, it defeats the purpose of a carefully crafted online image. Most blogs lack trustworthiness when it comes to establishing their ideas as authoritative on their issue. Most blog owners have no idea what they are doing to themselves. They are slowly committing social and professional suicide. Additionally, the target audience will "consider the source" when evaluating the nature of the content. If people see your website as a Joe's blog on everything, they will automatically assume you are ranting.

The nature of your personal website is to promote you, which will give people a reason to pause and consider the information on your website. Information on your website will be suspect to begin with because you are the source and the information is about you. You're biased and you should be. And they know it. People are very capable of detecting motive.

You should always put yourself in the best light possible. However, it is important when you create an online image that you are honest with the information you put out on the Internet. Being dishonest with your online image is the equivalent of lying on your resume. All of the hazards that exist when you lie on your resume are magnified when you lie on the Internet. Because you intend to eventually interact with the person that is checking out the information you place on the Internet, you need to be able to back up the goods.

A word of caution, there is a fine line that can be crossed when it comes to online credibility with your website. The right types of information will be informative and useful, while giving someone a feel for who you are. However, this information if overdone, can make your website appear like a hyped up sales pitch. More importantly, an over hyped image will not hold up in interviews and on the job so it's important to make your image an accurate representation of your capabilities.

With credibility on the Internet, awareness of the issue will help the development of your online image. Understanding how people make the determination of credibility will go a long way to building a useful online image. Making the appropriate decisions (e.g., not plagiarizing) when it comes to content of your online image will help create the credible online image you seek.

GAINING EXPOSURE OF YOUR ONLINE IMAGE

You've crafted your message and are ready for the world to see it. You only have one problem, how are you going to get people to see your message? After all, the Internet is a vast behemoth. In something that large, it would be easy to never be found. Your traditional choices for promotion or marketing of your message would be to advertise or spread by word of mouth activities. Yet, of all the millions of websites, your newly created one, isn't that important for word of mouth to spread news about your website. Additionally, I'm going to make an assumption that you do not have the financial resources to make a nationwide push to advertise your website in every media outlet.

Fortunately, the Internet community has a solution to the problem of finding information. Search engines make it possible to find your website by attempting to visit all websites on the Internet. Without search engines, your website is a needle in a haystack. These search engines look at the content of a website and categorize the relevance of the web pages for various search phrases. When a user searches for information on the Internet, the various web pages that are relevant to those search terms show up in the results pages. The higher you can get your webpage to appear in the search results, the more relevant and greater exposure you have gained for your online image. With Online Image Management, to gain exposure you are going to make efforts to manipulate the search results for key phrases which you will identify.

We will deploy techniques to ensure your intended links will show up in search engine results. In order to show up on the search engine results page you have several options. First, your website will need to have a URL that is highly relevant to your name. Second, you need to create a highly relevant web site for your targeted search terms. Third, you need to a "web" of websites that link back to your main website. These websites do not need to belong to you, they just need to link back to you. Fourth, you will submit your website to search engines for crawling. Finally, you will need to track how you appear in search engine results. Without tracking your progress you won't know if your efforts have been rewarded. These efforts combined, will make your website show up higher in search engine results thus increasing your exposure to the world.

PROTECTION OF YOUR ONLINE IMAGE

Once you have gone to the effort to create an image and get it exposed, the last problem you have deal with is protection of your image. As of this point in time, you probably won't have to worry about generating content that is going to hurt you, however, your past online image will need to be dealt with. You will need to eliminate the information that doesn't suit your purposes. Through various techniques you will need to get rid of the offending content. This will be easier if you own it or are on good terms with the creator of the content. Otherwise, you will need to take additional steps to get rid of negative image information.

Your website will serve as the place where you can deal with scandal. Hopefully you won't ever have to do it, but it will be the best way to deal with something you can't contain through normal measures. It gives you the opportunity to share your side of the story.

To generate a useful online image we need to transform your current image into a more useful image. You need to create a message that holds true to who you are, while at the same time, not shooting yourself in the proverbial foot. Some of the information that is out on the Internet might be neutral and not affect your online image. In that case, we will probably leave it alone. Examples of this, could be product comments or telephone directories. The determination of whether or not the information is neutral will depend on you, of course. You will have to deal with problems areas of your image in the protection aspect of Online Image Management.

OVERVIEW OF THE ONLINE IMAGE MANAGEMENT PROCESS

To meet the challenges of credibility, establishment, exposure, and protection associated with creating an online image, a new approach needs to be implemented. Online Image Management is broken down into six distinct phases. These phases are structured so that each phase builds upon the previous.

Online Image Management Phases

- ❧ Identification Phase

- ❧ Conception Phase

- ❧ Build Phase

- ❧ Promotion Phase

- ❧ Protection Phase

- ❧ Maintenance Phase

---

1 - IDENTIFICATION PHASE

In the first phase, you need to identify who you currently are on the Internet. You will go through the process of finding the information that exists currently on the Internet. This is a vital step so you know where you currently stand. What we are attempting to do is allow you to gain an understanding of your environment where you will be building your online image. In order to carry out the subsequent steps, you will need to know if you have to counteract what is currently out on the Internet.

You will start out by identifying what your current image is.   In order to find out what your image is, you will use the tools that people who don't know you will use. (In other words, if you don't know how to use Google, you soon will.) Additionally, you will chart your social network. We go through this step to identify what those people who could help and harm you at the same time. By applying the search techniques that you had previously used on yourself you will be able to find out the image of your close family and friends. We are only concerned with their image if they have tied themselves to you by linking or posting to your information. Or conversely, if you have tied yourself to their information thus associating your image with theirs.

Further in this process we will identify namesakes that you have out on the Internet. These are people who share your, hopefully, good name. These people are, in a sense, your competition. When it comes to image management, these are the people that will be try-ing to outdo your efforts to rank higher in the search engine results. More importantly, if they have a negative image you will need to distin-guish yourself from them. You don't want to inadvertently take credit for their misdeeds. That just isn't fair to you or them.

At the conclusion of this phase you will have a better idea of who you are on the Internet. For some people this will be an "oh crap" moment for them. When you recognize that you have this type of dirty image it can be troubling. Because you have read the book to this point, you know what can happen when you have a dirty image. Those of you that have an "oh crap" image, don't worry. By the time we are finished, those "oh crap" elements will have gone the way of the dodo bird.

For most people, their image will be a relatively clean slate. This recognition that they have no image should come with the knowl-edge that it isn't a bad place to be. Hopefully, you will be working with a clean slate. But if not, there are techniques we will use in latter phases that will help with a dirty image.

2 - CONCEPTION PHASE

The conception phase builds upon the identification phase. The second step in Online Image Management focuses on how you want to present yourself to the online world. In this conception phase, you will determine who you are *going* to be online. In a sense, you are conceiving your new online image. It's an opportunity for you to be reborn. An opportunity to reinvent yourself the way you want to be seen. No longer do you have to be pigeonholed in your life. You are now in the driver's seat and it's time for you to steer the direction of your online image.

Taking the information that you have acquired in the previous step you will do an analysis of your current image. You will analyze who you are in your real life in terms of the image you want to build on the Internet. What you will be looking for are the strengths and weaknesses you have. This knowledge will be the basis for improving your online image where you play up your strengths while minimize your weaknesses.

One of the first activities will be to draw the distinction between your exposed life and your private life. You will do this in order to maintain a sense of privacy. Let people see what you want them to see and nothing more. There is no need to expose every skeleton in the closet and frankly it's no one's business. You will want to make certain that you keep what you hold sacred and dear to you off the public forum of the Internet. This may mean that you want to keep your children and spouse off your online image. This distinction will be important because it will help you in determining content for your website later on.

Next, you will want determine which stereotype you will want to fulfill. This stereotype will be the foundation for who you are online. As such, all content you place on the Internet will support and build this stereotype. In effect, you are choosing to build upon a stereotype to enhance your own image. People want to see who you are and all you are doing is making sure they get the point of who exactly you are.

To develop your stereotype, you will do research on what other leading professionals in your field are doing. You will be looking for examples of model online images. Rather than reinvent the wheel, you can improve the wheel. If someone has managed to create a good online image, it would be a shame to let their work go to waste. Now, let me be perfectly clear, I am not advocating stealing their work. I am however, advocating that you learn from what they have done and figure out what has made their image effective as a professional in their field.

You're going to want to tie yourself to other professionals in the field. Ideally, you will have networking contacts already in your field that you will want to name drop. By name dropping, you will want to associate yourself with them in order to strengthen your credibility. You will want to link them into your map a social network that you want to expose as being connected to you.

In determining your stereotype that you want to fulfill you will want to carefully consider who you are in your real life. If you are an electrical engineer, wouldn't you want people who view your web content to see you as an electrical engineer? Of course you would, which is precisely why you focus on stereotype. Now if you are an electrical engineer looking for romance I recommend not building a website that could enhance your image as a "fighter pilot". While tempting to use the Internet to help you out in this aspect of your life, you should only portray yourself as a fighter pilot if you really are one. I don't recommend being dishonest about who you are. This course of action would destroy your creditability which is one of the key challenges of Online Image Management. Additionally, these sorts of untruths have a funny way of coming around. Call it karma if you will. It's much better just to elaborate on who you actually are and want to be. I suppose one could argue that if you were building your online reputation to get the guy or girl, the retaining love might be worth the expense to your professional life. But seriously, lots of people find electrical engineers sexy. OK, well some people do. OK. Well, this lady I know does. OK. Maybe it was her friend.

The stereotype you choose in this section will ultimately determine the remaining phases. The build phase and promotion phases depend heavily on what stereotype you want to promote. Further, your efforts at determining and crafting your message will be made easier by effort you put out in the conception phase of Online Image Management.

3 - BUILD PHASE

In the build phase, you will apply the concept of who you are online and put it into practice. Drawing upon the prior phases, you will have a clearer path for determining the type of content you want to place on the Internet. You will create a website for your message on the Internet. Your website will be the closest thing the Internet has to offer as the digital representation of you. The end result of this phase is to have a fully functional website. I wish I could tell you that it can be done in five minutes. But, as of this point in time, it really can't be done so quickly. It needs to be created and manicured.

To build a website, you will need to contract with a professional web designer. There are places to be cheap in this life, like at swap meets and at the gas pump, however, the design of your website is not one of them. It's important to get a good product at the end of this process. I certainly do not want to belittle your friend's twelve year old brother, Bobby, who also builds websites when he's not playing World of Warcraft. I do, however, want you to have a great online image and Bobby probably can't deliver what you need. No offense Bobby. There are too many technical issues involved with building a website to give the effort justice in this book. This book isn't a how to build a website, it's a how to build an online image. Leave the building to the professionals and the game playing to Bobby.

While some people will be able to do it themselves, this book's focus will be limited to educating you so you can make informed decisions. All technical issues related to the build phase will be to help you as an online image manager. I will include information that will educate you to the issues associated with building a website that you will need to provide input to the web designer.

In this phase, you will start to create the structure for content you want on your website. This will be basis for how you organize the message on your website.   Typically this structure will form the categories of content you provide on your website.   The content will include your resume, projects you've worked on, sections about you and your interests, et. c.

Once you create the structure of content, you will need to write the content for your website. You will need to write all content, because a web designer can't really write about you the way you can.   A web designer is there to provide you technical expertise not help with your message.   Your efforts in this area will be to optimize your message by creating scan-able pages to help people read them when they find your pages.

At the end of this phase, you will have a website that will be the best representation of you available on the Internet.   While this is an exciting step in your online image development, you need to get the word out on the Internet.   You will need to announce yourself to the world.

4 - PROMOTION PHASE

Announcing yourself to the world sounds like fun and it is. In this phase, you will tie other websites to your own as well as take advantage of other free website services. Through the creation of a strong network of websites, your online image will gain the credibility it needs to be a strong voice for you.

Using social networking websites can be very beneficial to your online image if done right.   Providing profile information that enforces your online image, at the same time redirecting to your website, enhances your online image.   In addition to the social networking websites, you will use companies that allow you to comment on products or articles.   What this allows you to do is show that you are active in your fields and builds your credibility for who you say you are.

You will need to integrate your online image into your real life. (No, I'm not talking about going out and taking flight school lessons. I'm referring to advertising your online image when you interact with the targeted audience.)   Placing your URL on your resume, your cover letters, your business card, e-mail signatures, and phone number slips. Further, you will go to the effort of linking to the organizations and products you feel promote your image.   If I were a software developer, I would want to link to professional software developer social networks.   Also, I would want to review books I have read on Amazon, so people can see I am a professional after all.

The promotion phase is there to do exactly what it says, to promote you.   To that end, if you have done an adequate job, people will be able to see your online image when searching for it.   Keep in mind, this phase never really ends.   It's a cycle which you will always be on the lookout for new ways to promote yourself.   Through promotion, your online image will be available for the world to see.   Now, all that's really left is to keep up the good work and prevent other people from undoing all of your hard work.

5 - PROTECTION PHASE

Perhaps one of the most intriguing elements of Online Image Management is the protection of what you have created.   The protection phase is intended to be what you do when threats occur to your online image.   Threats to your online image come in many forms. Threats such as a new competitor coming on to the scene looking to debunk your stranglehold on the top ten search results will be dealt with by revisiting the promotion phase.   Additionally, new advancements in technology make your website obsolete and require you to respond accordingly.

People often feel helpless when it comes to the Internet in

terms of getting rid of content. I'm here to tell you, you can repair your online image. When it gets interesting is how you can deal with threats that can destroy your online image altogether. Some people bought this book because they had a negative experience with something they, or someone from their social network, put online come back to bite them. These threats include the dreaded nude pictures, sex tapes, or drunk night partying pictures, as well as, ex's trying to destroy your good name. If you control the source of these images, or blogs, then you have some simple solutions, you can destroy them or ask them to be removed. Depending on the nature of the objectionable material, you may have to deploy measures to defend your online image. There will be multiple pathways to destroying this type of content and depending on the threat of the information out there, you will have to choose accordingly. This is the most challenging aspect of Online Image Management because of the difficulty of removing bad content. Now, if you are on good terms with the person who posted said content, the removal of such content can be as simple as picking up the phone and explaining to them what you are trying to do.

If you are not on good terms with the person who posted the content, all is not lost. Fortunately for you, businesses aren't bound by the same rules that apply to governments when it comes to freedom of speech. While a government may guarantee your detractor's freedom of speech, businesses have no such obligation. The business that hosts your detractor's website can also decide not to host the website if there is a violation of the terms of service. It is also possible to have these companies remove content that you find objectionable. All you have to do is make it worth their while to get rid of the content and this phase will cover how to do it. For those companies that will do nothing to help you out in your quest for the perfect online image, you don't have to get rid of the objectionable content. You just have to make the content irrelevant. You can do this by burying this content so deep in search results, few would ever be able to find it. Or you can address it head-on on your website, depending on the nature of the material.

6 - MAINTENANCE PHASE

The Internet is a living and breathing thing. It is constantly changing and as such, you will need to monitor it to find out what information is out there about you. After you complete the construction of your online image, you will need to go into the maintenance phase. Not paying attention to this aspect of Online Image Management will erode your hard work of creating an image in the first place. Only through monitoring can you get a feel for your online image as it exists today and tomorrow. This is going to be where you go through the identification steps periodically to ensure that nothing is cropping up.

In this phase of online image development, you will keep your information about you fresh and up to date. Through blogging or refreshing your design of your website from time to time, you will be able to keep the appearance of freshness on your website. You will also look for new trends in the Internet world and figure out how to take advantage of them to promote yourself. New trends can be a powerful way to promote yourself in ways other people are still adapting to. This is a way to solidify your online image and make you much more competitive than the competition. When you are the leader in Online Image Management, you can take the opportunity to make others react to your actions.

Additionally, you will use this monitoring phase to identify threats to your online image. You will have to monitor your namesakes to make certain that they aren't pulling a fast one on you. Early identification of troubling information will help you contain the damage. Only through monitoring of your online image, will you be able to know that it exists. When such threats are identified, you will need to utilize the protection phase of Online Image Management. Only through proactively going after threats will you be able to contain the damage.

SUMMING IT ALL UP

While Online Image Management is a challenging process, it's definitely worth doing. You will be reaping the rewards years to come. Being able to compete in the long haul with whoever you are competing will be invaluable to you. From better job offers to better dates, there isn't any aspect of your social life that won't be benefited by creating an online image.

CHAPTER SIX

IDENTIFICATION PHASE OF ONLINE IMAGE MANAGEMENT

"Observe all men; thy self most."

—Benjamin Franklin, American Founding Father

You are on your way to managing your online image. In the identification phase, you will be putting on the detective hat. You will be doing quite a bit of detective work in discovering who you are online. Your goal is to find all of the information that can be identified as you. To track down so much information in the online world you will need to organize yourself in order to sort through the information about you.

The process for this phase is fairly straightforward. First, you will be gathering potential targets for searching on you and your social network. You will write down information that would be useful in searching for your online image. To accomplish your goal you will establish a hit list of people you want to check out.

Secondly, you will scour the Internet for information about you.

You will be building a profile of your current image by collecting various tidbits of information about you from all over the Internet. Making sure that you list all sites where you are mentioned.

Thirdly, you will be checking up on the people you listed on your hit list. After all, a good way to get to find out information about you will be through your acquaintances. Besides, a little snooping can't hurt can it?

Finally, after you have tracked down all the information you can, you will need to make sense of it. What you want to determine is what stereotype are you currently on the internet. More importantly, you will determine if the information on the internet shows characteristics that are commonly associated with negative stereotype. In the end, you will have tracked down your current online image. Now let's get started.

FINDING YOUR ONLINE IMAGE

Considering that you know the most information about yourself, you are the best resource you have to start uncovering your online image. When considering what types of information you need to see if you can find on the Internet you need to know what knowledge the targeted audience member has about you. If your likely targeted audience member is a potential romantic interest, he/she may only have your name, phone number and/or e-mail address. Of course, this information is enough to get anyone started. After all, the targeted audience member only needs to find one thing that gives them more information about you and then they are on their way to learning more.

Most people will be building their online image to support their careers and as such need to be concerned about more than a simple name search. A prospective employer holds a wealth of information about you to search with. When you consider the information that you supply a prospective employer, chances are an HR representative would be exhausted before using all the potential search terms that can be pulled from an application, resume, and cover letter.

So the first thing you need to grab when you are conducting a search on yourself will be the materials you would send to a targeted audience member. For instance, if you were conducting a job search you would want your resume, cover letter and a sample application for employment from your favorite employer. If you are having difficulty finding an application for employment, just search for "employment application" on the web. The information collected via those materials can be very useful in determining what information a prospective employer has about you.

WHERE TO LOOK

Opening up your favorite web browser and starting the search for your online image is an exciting time in your quest to manage your online image. You're finally starting to move from the academic to the practical aspects of Online Image Management. The only question you may be asking yourself is, "now what?" That is an extremely fair question. After all, the Internet is huge. Google claims to have visited more than 1 trillion unique web pages available on the Internet .(Source Official Google blog, http://googleblog.blogspot. com/2008/07/we-knew-web-was-big.html) To cover that much ground you're going to need to turn to search engines.

But which search engine should you use? After all, there are several search engines available on the Internet. Most of these search engines are very similar in operation. You, the user, enter in search criteria and get back web pages that correspond to your search criteria. The search results that are returned vary from search engine to search engine. However, a majority of the time, search engines return similar results for the same search terms.

Search engines crawl the same Internet, and the only distinguishing differences between them are: how many pages they index, the way they determine which pages get returned, and in what order (ranking) are the pages returned based on a search query. When you consider that the top 3 search engines in the United States have almost 90% of the market share for Internet searches, the selection of which web search engines to include in your online image search becomes easier. Google is the number one search engine in the United States with 65% of Internet searches followed by Yahoo! at 16%, and then Microsoft search technology, Bing.com, at 11%. With this kind of market coverage, it is hard to argue that you need to use any search engine other than the top 3 search engines. When you account for the fact that the major search engines have more web pages indexed than their competitors, attempting searches on the minor search engines doesn't seem to make much sense. The amount of effort to get that extra 10% of search engines doesn't make it worth your effort. Thus, you only need to perform your online image search on Google, Bing, and Yahoo!.

When searching, you will want to go past the first page results. Typically, in one page of results there are ten web pages to review. The order or ranking these results are returned in is important because it shows relevance to your search criteria. Research shows that people generally only visit the first two pages of a search engine's returned results. So for any given search, they are only checking out the top 20 results. For the purposes of Online Image Management, you will want to go one step further and collect the top 30 rankings or the first 3 pages, whichever comes last.

You may still be tempted to try to include the smaller search engines in your coverage. I don't mean to dissuade you from searching with the smaller search engines. Many of the smaller search engines are constantly trying to move up and may provide you with various looks at your online image. Additionally, a case could certainly be made to use industry specific search engines if the industry you work in has industry specific search engines. For our purposes though, it is sufficient to cover the engines where the majority of your target audience is going to look to find information about you.   If you do choose to include the minor search engines, it will only cost you time and effort.

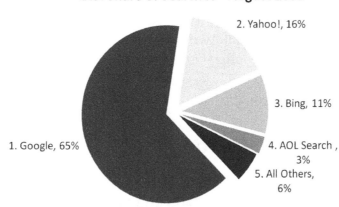

U.S. Share of Searches - August 2009

1. Google, 65%
2. Yahoo!, 16%
3. Bing, 11%
4. AOL Search , 3%
5. All Others, 6%

Nielson Online Internet Ratings, www.Nielson-netratings.com

SEARCHING THE SOCIAL NETWORKING WEBSITES

Don't look now, but another social networking website just launched.   In all seriousness, keeping up with the various social networking websites can be a tedious task.   It seems as if companies keep launching them one after another to cash in on the Web 2.0 Internet boom.   In order for you to keep up with these companies, your best bet is to rely on search engines to index them. For the most part these social network websites are well indexed by search engines.   An extensive search using all of the search terms you generate will not be necessary.

However, it is worth the time to take a look into the top two social networking sites (Facebook and MySpace) and search to see if you or your namesakes have a presence on these sites. The social networking sites typically have excellent tools to help you find the person you are looking for. After all, it is their business to help you connect with people inside your social network. You need to only search by your name. You probably already know which social networking websites you are active on so searching by your name might seem fruitless. However, you will potentially find namesakes by searching through the social networking websites. Knowledge of these namesakes will be beneficial later in the Online Image Management process.

WHAT TO SEARCH FOR

Ultimately, your target is to control how you appear when someone searches for you. However, to get there you need to perform the searches that you would expect your targeted audience to use as search criteria. Seeing how you appear on various search engines based on particular search criteria is an invaluable resource in determining what your online image is. Various search engines use different algorithms to return data based on your search criteria which is why you need to search through the top three search engines, Google, Bing, and Yahoo!.

Your goal is not to uncover the nuances associated with the various search engines but only how your online image appears in the top search results for your search criteria. Your search criteria will consist of pieces of information which can be gleaned from sources that you give out to prospective target audience members. These pieces of information range from your resume to your contact information like your phone number.

The search criteria recommend below is not intended as an all inclusive list, but rather a starting point for you to start tracking down your online image. This information is commonly grabbed from sources that you use to advertise yourself. It will be the source that someone like a prospective employer will use to track down your online image. It would be handy while you are constructing a list of search criteria that you want to perform on your image that you have your resume handy.

Sample List of Search Terms for John Jacob Jinglehiemer-Schmitt

Description	Search Term Example
Full Name (First Middle Last)	John Jacob Jinglehiemer-Schmitt
First and Last Name (First Last)	John Jinglehiemer-Schmitt
Reversed Name (Last First)	Jinglehiemer-Schmitt, John
Previous Names	John Jones
Nicknames	JDawg Schmitt
e-mail address on resume	jj@ JohnJacobJinglehiemer-Schmitt.com
Any other e-mail address you use	bigkahuna@anymail.com
Phone Number on resume	(123) 555-1234
Cell Phone Number on resume	(123) 555-6789
Phone Number you give out to friends and family	(123) 32JDAWG
Your Name plus College(s) Attended in quotes	John Jacob Jinglehiemer-Schmitt "Inkom Tech College"
Your Name plus High School(s) Attended in Quotes	John Jacob Jinglehiemer-Schmitt "Springfield High School"
Your Name plus organizations you belong to	John Jacob Jinglehiemer-Schmitt "NRA"
Your home address	123 EZ Street, Springfield, AnyState 12345 USA
Your Name plus your job titles	John Jacob Jinglehiemer-Schmitt "Lead Software Manager"
Your Name plus company	John Jacob Jinglehiemer-Schmitt "JJJ-Schmitt Software"

SEARCH BY NAME

Using variations of your name when searching will help identify web pages and documents that could have your information on them. To the target audience member, if they find your name in a document or webpage, they will immediately assume that they have found something that requires further investigation. They will need to inspect the page or document that was found in order to determine if information found on the page or document belongs to you.

Think of varying ways your name might be out on the Internet. By convention, a last name, first name approach to listing people is a very common way to present several people in a roster-like fashion. Additionally, people will often be referenced by their first and last name only as it is common to omit the middle name. Your culture in which you live may have common contractions for names such as Bob for Robert or Steve for Stephen. If you have this type of situation, you may want to add these common contractions to your list, especially if you tend to go by the contraction in informal settings.

Without a doubt, you should include previous names that you have used. Often employment applications require people to list previous names that they have gone by. If you have a maiden name, you will want to perform the same sort of searches with your maiden name.

SEARCH BY NICKNAME

A nickname often implies a sense of casualness. If you have material on the Internet that can be found with your nickname, it has a good likelihood of being information you don't want found on the Internet. Searching by nickname can be fruitful if you go by your nickname with your friends or if you use your nickname when you post on the Internet. A unique nickname such as "LightningBoyFan6779" is more easily attributed to you than a common nickname such as "Tomboy". Nicknames can be easily gleaned from login names, e-mail addresses or social network contacts.

SEARCH BY LOGIN CRITERIA

Searching by common user ids that you use is a good way to track down things you might have posted under a login ID. While you might think these sorts of things can't be found by someone who has your resume, you might be surprised. Furthermore, you may get to a point where after you are on the job, your employer may perform searches based on having a better idea of identifying criteria for you.

SEARCH BY PHONE NUMBER

This should be a quick search, but definitely worth your time to do so. While you won't find many results by your phone number, since most people are cautious with their phone number, information that has your phone number is immediately attributable to you. Phone numbers typically belong to a person or family at the most. This supposed unique relationship that all of us share with our phone numbers makes the information found with your phone number appear as belonging to you.

SEARCH BY E-MAIL ADDRESS

The e-mail address should be something that everyone searches for. The e-mail address is often used as login user id for many websites and comment boards. Like a Social Security number, e-mail addresses are immediately attributed to you because of the assumed unique relationship between person and e-mail address. If your e-mail address is on the Internet, that information belongs to you no matter what you say. Since e-mail addresses are unique, the returned results from the search engine should have your e-mail address in them.

SEARCH BY SCHOOLS YOU ATTENDED

Educational background is regularly requested on applications and resumes. An employer wishing to verify claims of education can check up on you with this technique. Some educational institutions have a nasty habit of posting alumni on their websites. By including the name of your school that you attended and your name, an employer can find out if you attend the school. Additionally, some schools will allow people to look for lost classmates via their website or have discussion boards in which you can write notes to your other classmates. This just opens up a can of worms that you don't want to have to deal with. Furthermore, you never know if something you told a college newspaper made its way on to the Internet unbeknownst to you.

SEARCH BY ORGANIZATIONS YOU BELONG TO

Unless you have listed these on your application, an employer will probably not conduct this search. However, some organizations post rosters of membership as a way to show they aren't just a couple of people who got together one late night to form a club. Albeit absolutely fine for an organization to do so, if your name is included on a roster of a politically incorrect organization you may pay the consequences of belonging to that group.

THINGS TO AVOID SEARCHING BY

As a general rule, you should not search with any search term you wouldn't be comfortable putting on a postcard and sending to your grandmother who lives across the country. There are some search terms that should not be used under any circumstances. Search terms such as your social security number, credit card numbers, et. c. would qualify as terms that should not be searched with. The reasons for not searching with this type of data range from the way data is sent to search engines to the way your browser stores data. Most search engines do not add the encryption necessary to protect the information as it is being transmitted over the Internet. You can't blame search engine companies for taking this stance. Search engines do not encrypt data over the Internet because, for the most part, most search terms do not need the protection of encryption. Additionally, encryption is very expensive in terms of speed when you process tens of thousands of searches per second.

The nature of the Internet makes these search terms available in the logs of any network device that happens to pass along the message. As such, any of these logs could be read by multiple people. Furthermore, Internet browsers have a nasty habit of storing search term data for later use. If someone were to get on your computer after you were on it, your data could be stolen. There are just too many reasons why you shouldn't search by these search terms.

MAKING SENSE OF WHAT YOU FOUND

Potentially, you will be uncovering several websites while looking for your online image. The number of websites that you find could get quite difficult to keep track of, if you don't keep records about each one. You will also want to keep track of where you found the link to the information about you.   By keeping track of this up-front, it will be easier to check up on your current image over time when you have forgotten about how you got to this page in the first place.   If you found the link on a search engine, what was the page ranking of the search engine.   The page ranking will indicate likelihood of someone finding the information.   Further, this initial snapshot of where the page ranked will be helpful if you need to track the page ranking over time.

You will want to write a brief description of why you think this is linkable to your image.   This will be helpful to refer to later when you are trying to piece together your online image.   The brief description needs to remind you why you felt the information was attributable to you in the first place.   If it's obvious why something is attributable to you, then your description will be very brief.

One way to keep track of this information is to print out the web page and attach a description sheet.   Using a description sheet you can jot down the information you want to keep track of and have a physical copy of the web page.   Additionally, you will have a snapshot in time of the website in its current state.

The important task is making sure that you can keep it straight when you need to assess your image.   Make notes about the overall credibility of the site that you can refer to later.   These notes will help you make determinations when you will need to classify what your online image is.   You may want to bookmark each of the pages as well.

DETERMINING IF AN ITEM IS NEGATIVE OR NEUTRAL

You need to determine if the information you found can impact your online image. To make this important classification, you need to conduct an image-impact test. To conduct this image-impact test, you will ask yourself a series of questions.   If you find that you answer yes to any of the following questions, classify the page as negative.

Classifying the Web Page as Negative or Neutral

- Would you want your parents, spouse, children, and / or grandparents to see this webpage?

- Does this information conflict directly with your resume.

- Would an employer fire you if they found this information on the Internet?

- Would an employer not hire you if they found this information on the Internet?

- Would the girl or guy of your dreams refuse to date you if they found this information?

- Did you leak corporate secrets accidentally on the Internet?

- Could what be found on the Internet be used against you in a court of law?

- Could someone use this information to illegally discriminate against you? For instance, does the information contain information regarding sexual or religious orientation?

- Does the information expose members of your social network that you want to keep hidden from view?

Everything else label as neutral for now. Until you know who you want to be online, don't worry about a deeper classification for the pages. In the next phase, we will further classify this information to determine whether or not it belongs in your online image.

IDENTIFYING OTHER CRAFTERS OF YOUR ONLINE IMAGE

We need to gather information about people who are potential contributors to your online image. Content created by other people who could be tied to you is an often overlooked component of an online image. Most people seemingly don't care what their friends do on the Internet until it affects them directly. However, you want to identify people whom you are easily connected via your social network. Since you don't control who can publish content, you're going to need to check on the most likely people who could publish content about you. The people who publish content within your inner circle of your social network will be people you need to monitor their publishing efforts on the Internet.

You may be tempted to rush off to speak with people you know who are writing content out on the Internet immediately about the potential damage they could cause you. You should be cautious when speaking to them about your online image. If, for some reason in the future, you are on the outs with your family member, it may come back to haunt you as they realize a way to get back at you. As such, they might attempt to undermine your efforts in Online Image Management. The best policy for right now is to avoid speaking with people about your online image until you have a better idea of what you want your online image to be. After all, you may want to purposefully expose them as being in your online image if it helps your overall image.

MAKING YOUR HIT LIST

This isn't the gangster style hit list. This is an online image hit list. Essentially, it is a list comprised of people you need to check out to make sure they aren't actively blogging or social networking. At most, you will need to create a list of up to twenty people. Any more than twenty people on your hitlist would be difficult and tedious.

(But if you feel the need to profile more of your social network, don't let me stop you.) For some people this list could be exhaustive, for others, not so much. What you are trying to do is create a manageable list of likely suspects.   You don't want to put the paper boy down on your list, unless you've owed him two dollars for a long time. But, if you feel a bit down about having only two people on your list, you could create some imaginary friends.

Characteristics of a Hit List Candidate

- They likely have or have had access to you on an ongoing basis either through in person meetings or over the Internet.

- You see them more than once every six months.

- They are on a first name basis with you.

- They use the Internet.

- If the spirit moved them, they could write something about you.

- They may be able to produce pictures of you and them together. (This means any picture. It doesn't matter whether or not they are incriminating.)

- This person has a strong positive or negative opinion about you. Passion often leads people to do things they otherwise wouldn't do. People with strong positive emotions about you may write things that tie you to them on their blog, whereas people with strong negative opinions about you may do things to destroy you in a passive aggressive fashion over the Internet.

- They may be or have been a coworker, subordinate, or someone who at some point in their life took direction from you.

THE APPLE DOESN'T FALL FAR FROM THE TREE PEOPLE - YOUR FAMILY

To start off, add the obvious members of your inner circle to the hit list. Your family, especially your immediate family members consisting of your parents, your spouse if married, your in-laws, your siblings, your children, your grandparents (if Internet savvy), close aunts and uncles. What you will be checking is what kind of presence on the internet your immediate family members. While I am not suspecting that your immediate family members would have any reason to spread garbage about you, I want you to make certain that these family members don't have the type of presence that could hurt you if you were tied to them.

Think about how many ways your family can be tied to you. Social networking sites make a living connecting family members to your account. Further, the default settings on those sites will show who you're friends with. It doesn't take a genius to connect people with the same last name as related to you. Social networking aside, some families will post genealogical references on the Internet. While perhaps useful to the family member that posted the information, this type of information is not particularly beneficial to your Online Image Management efforts.

Along those same lines, many people create blogs and/or family websites with no regard to the information they are making publicly available. Many people are careful to not place information such as addresses and children names on the Internet, they simply don't realize that usually, there are enough pieces of information to tie the information to the blog to the respective family members. Unfortunately, most people lack the technical expertise to password-protect the blog or website to only family members who should see their online resource.

PARDON ME, HAVE YOU SEEN MY MISSING NOBEL PRIZE AROUND HERE ANYWHERE? – ROMANTIC INTERESTS

The difference between love and hate is a very thin line. A person could be your "one and only" one day and your "public enemy number one" the next. The Internet gives a megaphone to people who you have been romantically involved with. People who are connected to you via romantic means are particularly important to include on the hit list because of the deep connection they once shared with you. When emotion runs deep, people will do things they would not normally do. Several more prominent cases of online image destruction involve a past lover who had incriminating stories and/ or pictures. You will probably have an idea of which past lovers would go all out to destroy your online image. Add all relationships you have had within the past five years to the hit list. Pay particular attention to your past partners that they had a blog or website while you dated. There is nothing like the chronicles of finding the rise and fall of relationships. It should be treated privately and has no business in a public forum like the Internet.

If, in a moment of weakness, you have allowed yourself to be photographed, videotaped, or recorded in some other manner, in a compromising situation you will need to make certain you add the holder of the materials to your hit list in Capital letters. These potential slipups can ruin an online image and be particularly difficult to remove from the Internet.

BIRDS OF A FEATHER – YOUR FRIENDS

Your close friends can be one of the greatest sources for image destruction which automatically qualifies them for the hit list. The worst part is, most of the time your friends aren't spreading the seeds to your online image destruction maliciously. They are simply reporting to the rest of the world about the great time they had with you at the party the other night. Regrettably, to the suspecting targeted audience member who comes across the information, they take the information for face value. The targeted audience member does not factor in the apparent inside joke that you share with your friends about toilet humor. All the targeted audience member sees is the photograph of you straining on the toilet. The intent isn't important just that they are publishing information about you. It is just that friends are likely to have the opportunity to see you at your private moments and then want to embarrass you the best way they know how, over the Internet.

Unfortunately, your friends are even more likely to have the capability to record and capture you in incriminating photos. Depending on your relationship with your friends, some of them may purposefully put information out on the Internet to embarrass you. Friends seemingly do not understand how harmful these practical jokes can actually be.

THE PEOPLE YOU WANT PEOPLE TO ASSOCIATE WITH YOU – YOUR PROFESSIONAL REFERENCES

Another overlooked area of people to include on your hit list is your professional references. These are the group of people that you would include in any job application or resume. Professional references are important to review since you are exposing elements of your social network to your prospective employer. Your professional references will say as much about you as anyone. This is especially true since you obviously respect these people and assume they have a very positive opinion of you. If their online image is dirty, you will not want to include them as references because they can impact your overall image when applying for employment.

THE PEOPLE WHO WOEFULLY DESPISE YOU - YOUR ENEMIES

Finally, you need to add your enemies to the list.   These are the people who strive to make you look bad every chance they get. You may think you have no enemies but you need to carefully consider whether or not you have anyone out there that you have wronged that would want to do character assassination over the Internet on you. When you consider the motive for someone to take out their passive aggression against you on the Internet, you may uncover additional people.   For instance, if you are abrasive at work, or if you are rude to your next door neighbor, it might be all someone needs to motivate them to blog about you that night.   Even still, perhaps you stole somebody's significant other or didn't return their romantic gestures. When strong emotions like love are involved, it is hard to predict the behavior of the offended individual.

NARROWING DOWN THE LIST

After completing your hit list of people, you will want to go through and rank these people by the possible damage they could do to your online reputation.   Rank these people from 1 to 20, with the number 1 being the highest priority to research and 20 being the lowest priority for researching.   For time purposes, try to limit the search to the top 20.   If you want to go the extra mile and research everyone, go ahead. But keep in mind, the majority of searches that will turn up elements of your online image will be done via your searches for your own online image, not these hit list searches.

SEARCHING THE LIST

The hit list is going to give you an idea of who has enough of an Internet presence that if someone were able to tie the people on your hit list to you, it would give you reason for concern. The hit list gives you a starting place to assess whether or not your people on your social network can hurt or help you. The effort to search for people on your social network will not be as intensive as searching for elements of your own online image. The justification for narrowing the search is two-fold. For starters, it takes too much time to profile twenty people in as much depth as you have for your own image. Secondly, people who are seeking out your online image will not want to spend a lot of time tracking down your social network.

Sample List of Search Terms for hit list member – Janice Marie Hoozlefritz

Description	Search Term Example
Full Name (First Middle Last)	Janice Marie Hoozlefritz
First and Last Name (First Last)	Janice Hoozlefritz
Reversed Name (Last First)	Hoozlefritz, Janice
Previous Names	Janice Doe
Nicknames	JannyDoe
Your Name + Hit list Full Name	John Jacob Jingleheimer-schmidtt, Janice Marie Hoozlefritz

Conduct the search in the same fashion as you did with your own profile. Rank the web pages you find in the same fashion as you did your own online image. Rate the pages as neutral or negative depending on the list of questions you asked when you rated your own online elements.

STEREOTYPING YOUR CURRENT IMAGE

Learning to stereotype your image is a critical Online Image Management skill. What makes stereotype classification of your online image so important is the fact that people use stereotypes to judge who you are. In order to take advantage of this stereotyping behavior, you need to build your image to support the stereotype you want to take advantage of.

To determine your current image you are going to depend on yourself and someone who you would classify as an acquaintance or someone you hardly know but would be willing to take a look at your online image for you if you asked them.

Essentially you are going to depend on your own set of stereotypes which you hold, in order to determine what stereotype you have. As you start this process, you should briefly review the information you have collected so far. After reviewing this information, write down a few thoughts about who you are online. For instance, write down what you learned about you.

✓ Perhaps you found your employment history?

✓ Did you learn about any of your family members?

✓ Which people have exposed your social network?

✓ Is there a picture with you in it?

✓ How did the picture make you look?

✓ Could you tie yourself to your family members based of off the information found on the Internet.

✓ Did you learn anything personal about yourself? Maybe you like to play the flute or harp or collect model trains.

✓ Did you find information about past relationships?

Hopefully you like what you have seen so far about who you are on the Internet. At this point, you need to detach yourself from the process. You will need to be honest and clear about what you think about your image.

Now, you will want to create a list of five adjectives that you feel accurately describe the person you are online. Remember, there are no right or wrong answers here, it's just what you feel. Reflect upon the information you have written down and then write down your five adjectives.

After writing down your adjective list, imagine the person those adjectives describe. Write down the stereotype you feel embodies those five words (e.g., student, geek, loser, businessman / businesswoman, blond). Sometimes, it takes two or more stereotypes to accurately describe the information you have found. At this point in the process, you shouldn't worry about the number of stereotypes you embody. It will become more important as you create your online image, to narrow down the stereotypes that your online image promotes in order to provide clarity.

GETTING HELP UNCOVERING YOUR ONLINE IMAGE.

Often, we are too close to the trees to see the forest. Getting a second opinion of your current online image is quite useful. You need to find someone whose opinion you trust to review your current online image.   After all, your online image is in the eyes of the beholder. This person may be able to give you insight to your online image that you hadn't thought about. Further, they can apply their own set of stereotypes which can give you an idea of how other people see you online.

This person, let's call them your "online image helper" should be willing to spend some time in order to help you uncover your online image. Explain to your online image helper that what you need is a blatant, no holds barred, no sugar coated opinion of what they think about your online image. The more honest they are with their opinion of you the better off you are going to be in determining whether or not you were accurate in assessing your online image. You should not ask someone to review what you have profiled so far.

Let your online image helper review the pages on the Internet you found on their own. Ask them to write down a few words describing their impression as they visit each of the pages. You may want to schedule time when you can come back and review the pages with them so you can understand why they felt the way they did when they viewed each page. Ask them to tell you what they learned about you in the process. This is important because it will show you what stood out in their mind as they looked at your online image. Now, ask them to give five adjectives that describe the person they were looking at online. Write down their list so that you may refer to it at a later time. Then ask them to give you a stereotype that in their mind embodies who you are online. Finally, you should ask them if they feel that what they see online is a true representation of who they think you are based on your previous dealings with them.

Once you are finished with them, start asking yourself questions as to why they gave the adjectives they did. Did the adjectives match the ones you had listed? Did the stereotype match or at least come close to the one you came up with. If you can't seem to figure it out, you may want to contact them one more time to talk with them about the differences you had between your vision of your online image and their vision of your online image.

SUMMING IT ALL UP

At this point in the Online Image Management process, you have researched yourself and the top 20 people on your hit list. While you may be starting to have an idea of how your online image presents you over the Internet, you need to take some time to put it all together. You need to assess how this information shapes the stereotype of your online image. Finally, you have recruited the help of someone whose opinion you trust to evaluate your current online image.

The combination of the stereotype you labeled yourself as and the stereotype your online image helper labeled you as is your best indication of what your online image is. After reviewing your stereotype, take a moment to think about the information you were able to find on the Internet that you were able to directly control and the information that you did not place out there. For most, this can give a feeling of helplessness. It is as if you are in a small boat at the mercy of a stormy sea. If you are in this boat, guard against despair. Remember, begun is halfway done. You will be able to right the course of your online image and undo most of what has been done to your online image.

CHAPTER SEVEN

CONCEPTION PHASE OF ONLINE IMAGE MANAGEMENT

"Our self image, strongly held, essentially determines what we become."

—Maxwell Maltz, American Cosmetic Surgeon

Your mind is one of the most amazing creations that exist. Your mind, filled with its knowledge of social stereotypes, will help you immensely as you decide how to craft your online image. The mind has the capacity to understand stereotypes and apply them. Since your mind tends to absorb the concept of a stereotype and then make yourself into that stereotype, you need to make sure you choose a stereotype that embodies what you want to accomplish in your life.

In this phase of Online Image Management, you will determine the course of your online image. Additionally, you will be picking a stereotype to guide you. At the same time, we will address which aspects of your life to keep private and which areas to expose. At the end of this phase, you should have a clear understanding of what stereotype you are going to use to promote yourself over the Internet.

THE ABILITY TO ASSUME A STEREOTYPE

If we think of ourselves as a particular stereotype we tend to act that way. The famous Stanford prison experiment conducted in 1971 demonstrated the capability of our minds to craft how we see ourselves and our world. The experiment was meant to study the psychology of prison life. Twenty four volunteer college students from Stanford were screened for normalcy and then selected to take part in the experiment. At the toss of a coin, the students were split into two groups, guards and prisoners. The group of students, soon to be student-prisoners, were rounded up by squad cars and underwent a typical booking into prison experience. The group of student-guards received no training and where only told to assume the role of being a guard. The guards could set their own rules and were to maintain security in the prison.

The experiment was scheduled to last two weeks. However, the experiment had to be cut short due to safety concerns for the student-prisoners. While I don't need to go too far into the details of the experiment, just know that over the course of six days, the experiment had to be ended because of the degrading treatment of the student-prisoners at the hands of the student-guards. What happened was the student-guards and student-prisoners assumed their stereotypical role so well, the experiment became dangerous for the prisoners.

Keep in mind that these students were equals a mere six days earlier. Yet, at the end of the sixth day, these students had assumed their stereotypical role so well, you wouldn't have been able to distinguish them from real prisoners. Because we all share common stereotypes in our culture, we have very real knowledge of how a stereotype should act. (For more information on the Stanford prison experiment, visit the project's website, http://www.prisonexp.org or search for "Stanford Prison Experiment" on your favorite search engine.)

Although a very extreme example of assuming the role of a stereotype, the experiment relates to Online Image Management only to show you how well we all understand stereotypes and how easily we can apply a stereotype. We all understand stereotype so well that if any one of us were put into a prisoner/guard situation we would assume the role. Indeed, the ability to assume the stereotype will help you through the creation of an online image. In an online world, seeing yourself as the stereotype you pick will help you act online within the bounds of that stereotype.

THE NEED FOR CLARITY IN AN ONLINE IMAGE.

Clarity in your approach to presenting your online image is a necessary element of your online image. The ability to apply a clear stereotype online will make or break your online image. An approach that focuses on clarity improves the quality of the message being sent because it removes ambiguity from your message. A clear message improves the likelihood that the message was understood by the receiver. As an example of clarity, consider the saying: if a person sees something that quacks like a duck, walks like a duck, and flies like a duck, they will naturally conclude that they are in fact looking at a duck.

You want your message to be loud and clear. When you provide a clear online image, you are communicating very directly with the receiver of your message. What you are communicating is a strong message that you are what your online image says you are. You are telling the receiver that you see yourself as what the online image portrays you to be.

In order to present a clear stereotype, you need to make certain the characteristics you show online are consistent with the stereotype you are trying to display in person. You can do this by asking yourself before you put anything out on the Internet, "Does this truly reflect the stereotype that I am trying to promote?" By asking yourself that simple question, you will be avoiding problems most of the time. A simple rule should be, if you feel at all uneasy about what you are putting on the Internet, don't put it out there. You will sleep easier at night and likely come up with something better to put out there.

Indeed, nothing is more confusing to someone than a conflicting online image. When pieces of your image say you are a professional and other pieces of your online image say you are a partier, it is mostly up to the beholder of your image to determine what your online image is. It's the same concept that embodies the phrase that sleaze bags use, "Your mouth says no… but your body says yes". You definitely don't want to be on the other end of that saying. Accounting for human behavior, most people will give the negative material more weight when considering someone's online image.

YOUR GOALS FOR YOUR ONLINE IMAGE

Figuring out for yourself what the goal is for your online image is the most useful step in creating an online image. Identifying a clear goal of your online image will give you something to refer to when you are considering new ideas for your online image. You may be thinking at the moment you don't even know what you want to eat today, let alone what you want to be like in five years. While you may be right, most of us have some thoughts as to where we would like to end up. Further, most people that read this book are forward enough thinkers to identify at least one aspect of their life where a positive online image could improve their situation.

How you present your online image depends on what you want to accomplish with your online image. What people want to accomplish with their online image varies as much as people do. For some, an online image seeks to provide clarity about who they are and counter negative material on the Internet. For others, an online image will help maintain their current social status. And for a larger bunch, they want to use their online image to help them advance and reach life goals such as career advancement, dating success, and/or admission to select universities or organizations.

A worthy goal of an online image would be to help you accomplish a real life goal. Picking a goal for your online image such as, "I want my online image to help me get my dream job", will keep you motivated and on target. Remembering that we live in the real world and not the virtual world, goal attainment in real life is much sweeter than goal attainment on the Internet. After all, goal attainment in real life improves your life across the board.

To counter indecisiveness with your goals, focus on one area of your life you are most impacted by what people think of you. Maybe that area of your life is your career goals and maybe it is not. By focusing on the one area of your life, you will have an easier time deciding what your goal in that area should be. To identify the goal of your online image, consider an aspect of your life which would be improved with an online image. Perhaps you want to consider your career, or your love life as potential targets for your online image.

Once you determine you want to improve a particular aspect of your life, you need to ask yourself a series of questions.

- ✓ Does this aspect of my life depend on what other people think of me?

- ✓ Am I happy with the current state of where I am?

- ✓ Is there room for improvement in that aspect of my life?

- ✓ If this aspect of my life were perfect what would that aspect of my life be like?

- ✓ Is this improvement in that particular aspect of my life worth the effort of an online image?

- ✓ How will I know when I attain the stated goal?

- ✓ What would be the necessary steps I would need to take to achieve that goal?

When you create your goal, you should make certain that your goal avoids vagueness. Make sure that your goal is clear to you and can be easily measured. For example, a goal which states, "I want to use my online image to be rich in five years" may seem measurable to you. After all, at the end of five years you should be able to take stock and determine whether or not you made your goal of being rich. However, being rich today, may mean having a million dollars in your savings account.   In five years from now, being rich might mean you have fulfilling family relationships.

An example of a good goal would be something measurable, such as, "I want to use my online image to achieve a position with a company which would allow me to save $1,000,000 by January 15, 2020. This goal is great because it is time specific, measurable, and completely attainable. On January 15th, 2020 you will be able to sit down and see if you have 1 million dollars.

When you consider the time frame of your online image, you should realize that your online image is a work in progress. Setting milestones for your online image will help you keep on track. Milestones such as when you want your website to go live on the Internet and when you want to start evaluating your online image for effectiveness.

Once you determine your goal, you should realize that your online image is a tool to help you achieve your goal. Although your online image is an awesome tool to accomplish life goals remember that it is only a tool and not a substitute for a plan. A plan to reach your goals can and should involve use of an online image, but should be broadened to include other aspects of your life that need to be improved to attain your goals.

SELECT THE TARGET AUDIENCE

Since the Internet is accessible to most, the audience receiving your message can be anyone. While you don't know for certain who can access your online image, you should build to the audience which can impact you the most. The target audience member that could impact your life the most, largely depends on what you consider to be most valuable in your life. If you consider your friends to be most valuable, you would want to build a website that is highly friend centered. Rather, if you consider your employment most valuable, you will want to build your image to make you look the best in a professional light.

An online image needs to support your goal. Your goal communicates what your target audience should be. If your goal is to be married to Mr. Right within 5 years, then your targeted audience is all of the potential Mr. Right's in the world. Or perhaps your goal is to be a CEO of a major corporation within five years. If that is the case, then your targeted audience should be the professional recruiters for major corporations. Whatever your goal is, your targeted audience should be a natural extension of that goal.

When you start out in the world of Online Image Management you should avoid targeting multiple audiences with your online image. Although focusing on a single target audience restricts the ways you can present your image, it helps with clarity. Restricting yourself to a single target audience helps you limit your message to your single goal.

Lastly, when selecting your target audience you should identify someone who personifies your target audience. If you know someone who fits your target audience, this person could be a great resource. Having someone to imagine when you are thinking of a typical target audience member will help you further clarify your online image. However, if you do not know someone who personifies your target audience, picking a targeted audience member stereotype, like Mr. Right, can give you all the information you need to get started.

IDENTIFY THE STEREOTYPE YOU WANT TO PORTRAY

It's true, stereotypes tend to get a bad rap whenever a person mentions stereotyping. Something about the way our culture has pushed us to demonize the term stereotype has led us all to run quickly from the mere mention of the term. However, if you're going to build an online image, you had better get used to the concept of stereotyping. As discussed earlier in the book, stereotyping isn't a bad thing. Stereotyping is how we communicate very quickly as to the nature of a person or situation.

Political parties understand the power of stereotypes and have so for many years. Political campaigns attempt to make their candidate fit the mold of the office that they are running for. If their candidate is running for president, they want the electorate to see their candidate as a president. Conversely, by framing an opposing candidate as having nondesirable presidential characteristics such as being too old (made easier if they are in fact old), the hope of the campaign is we all quickly apply the stereotype of someone who is out of touch with normal Americans, and someone who yells at the TV.

Of course, your goal of Online Image Management isn't quite at the same level as a presidential campaign. Yet, your online image shares many of the same problems of a presidential candidacy. You need people to see you as someone who is capable of doing what you say you can do. Like a presidential candidate, you need to fit the mold in their mind of what they are looking for. Additionally, people need to see you as a person. The more they are able to relate with you the better they will feel about you.

Depending on your goals for an online image, there are two ways to construct the stereotype you want to promote over the Internet. You can choose a stereotype that reflects who you *currently are* over the Internet or you can choose a stereotype which reflects who you *want to be* in the near future. If you are happy with where you are at currently in your life and are only looking for an online image to enhance your life, then you should build an online image based on your current stereotype so that you don't give up the ground that you have gained.   Otherwise, if you want to use your online image for advancement of a particular area of your life where you want to improve, then you should evaluate what your current stereotype is and what it says about you.   Once you have clarified your current stereotype, you should build a stereotype that will get you to where you want to be.

If you choose to improve some areas of your life, you will use two stereotypes: one that is the current you and one that is the future you.   You need to take the two stereotypes and merge them together. Once merged, you will determine how many steps you need to take before you can attain the future goal.

FINDING YOUR CURRENT REAL LIFE STEREOTYPE

Yes, you already have an idea of what your current online image is based on the Identification phase. But before you are able to select a stereotype for your online image, take the time to find out what your *current stereotype is in real life*.   Knowing who you are is something that can take a lifetime to figure out.   But, since we don't have a lifetime to determine your stereotype, you're going to have to improvise.   You are going to need to make some generalizations about who you are.   Your current stereotype should be a true representation of you that puts you in the best light possible.

You can start out by looking at the aspect of your life that you want your online image to enhance.   If you want to showcase your career, you can reflect upon what you do for a living.   Choosing a stereotype from your career field will communicate several things about you which will be helpful to dictate the kind of things you need in an online image.   If you are the CEO of a non-profit company that makes wigs for children who have undergone chemotherapy, first of all, God bless you.   Second of all, the stereotype you currently are is of a compassionate CEO or entrepreneur.

Regardless of whether or not you are having difficulty determining a stereotype, usually the people who know you best can help you determine what stereotype best describes you. Turning to other people to help classify you with stereotype is not only effective but a wise recognition of what your stereotype is: a reflection of what *other* people think of you. Ask people you know to think of a single word that best describes you. This single word will give you insight as to what they think is your most glaring characteristic.

Next, you can ask them to outline your best and worst characteristics. Be careful though, once you open the flood gates for people to tell you what's wrong with you, you will have to take it all with a grain of salt and avoid critiquing their choice of attributes. If you criticize, you will not get the honest opinions you need to help you determine your stereotype. If you turn to other people, make certain that you ask for more than one opinion. Sometimes certain people might have a jaded opinion of you. Only by getting multiple opinions of your stereotype, can you feel as if you're current stereotype is accurate.

CHARTING A STEREOTYPE

Charting a stereotype is a useful tool to recognize the characteristics of a stereotype. Putting it down on paper, helps flush out the characteristics of a stereotype. To illustrate what a charted stereotype looks like, review the charted stereotype. To start with we put the label of the stereotype into our graph. In this case we have diagramed the stereotype of a marketing representative. Notice that on the left hand side of the page, the positive attributes of a marketing representative are listed.

When you chart your stereotype start by brainstorming about all of the positive attributes of your particular stereotype. These characteristics should come quickly to you, which will show that you understand the stereotype. Be specific with the descriptive words

CHARTED STEREOTYPE: MARKETING REPRESENTATIVE

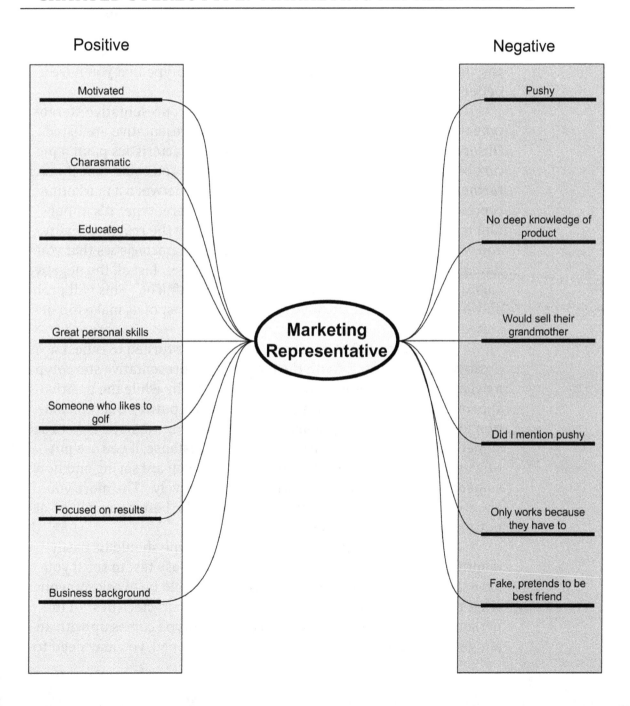

Positive

Motivated

Charasmatic

Educated

Great personal skills

Someone who likes to golf

Focused on results

Business background

Marketing Representative

Negative

Pushy

No deep knowledge of product

Would sell their grandmother

Did I mention pushy

Only works because they have to

Fake, pretends to be best friend

and phrases that you use to describe your online image. If you use vague descriptions they may be confused with another stereotype. The more you can nail down to very specific attributes, the more clarity you will be able to provide to the receiver of your online image message. If the attributes of your selected stereotype do not come easy to you, consider choosing a different stereotype that you have a better feel for.

On the right hand side of the marketing representative stereotype the negative attributes of a marketing representative are listed. Observe that the marketing representative characteristics paint a picture of a typical bad marketing representative. You could take it much further, but then there would be no distinction between a marketing representative and a demon. With your own stereotype, it's important to keep your negative characteristics within the realm of reality. You want to make certain that you do not list characteristics that you have no chance of including in your online image. List all the negative characteristics of the stereotype that you can think of. This will probably be easier than the positive aspects since most of us make fun of stereotypes with our humor.

Keep in mind that negativity can often be turned to reflect a positive characteristic. With the marketing representative stereotype, a negative characteristic is someone who is pushy while the positive spin on that characteristic is a go getter. When putting out information for your online image consider how someone might be able to see something as a negative characteristic. For instance, if you are putting up a posting on a website, consider what you are saying and how someone might take what you are saying negatively. The more you are able to consider a different point of view, the better you will be at putting out information that helps you.

All of the characteristics of your stereotype should be easily identifiable with your current stereotype. An easy test to see if you have the characteristics correctly identified would be to ask someone what they think of as you read them all of the characteristics. If the person you ask to identify your charted stereotype comes up with an altogether different stereotype than you envisioned, you may need to get a second opinion. Like most things, practice makes perfect when it comes to correctly characterizing a stereotype. Further refinement might be necessary to get your stereotype right.

   With your online image, you are going to want to promote yourself as the positive attributes only. However, you will need to make the determination as to whether or not which attributes are positive based on your view of the stereotype. This way you will be happy with the way you decided to present yourself and more likely to live up to the expectations put upon yourself by your stereotype.

BUILDING A STEREOTYPE WHICH WILL HELP YOU MEET FUTURE GOALS

   To build the online image which meets your future goal, you are going to need to pick the future stereotype that you want to use as the source of your online image. This future stereotype will be what you see your stereotype as when you achieve your life goal. In order for you to achieve that goal, you need to assume characteristics of the future stereotype. You will need to assume the role with your online image and behave online in a manner fitting of your future stereotype.

   The principal you will be applying to your online image is that you dress for success. In other words, you need to look the part before you get the part. For instance, if you are a marketing representative who wants to be the vice president of marketing, you probably need to be seen as someone who understands marketing and is very effective at the art of marketing. If you embody those traits already, but haven't been given the opportunity to showcase your talents then your online image is a perfect place for that. However, if you are still in the process of developing those traits then you would want to create a plan for getting you to those steps. Seeing yourself in the role of a vice president of marketing, can help you act as a vice president of marketing would. However, unless you have taken action to prepare yourself for the next level, most people are not going to see you as what you want to be seen as.

If you are at the stage in your career where you are gifted at what you do, in this case marketing, you should have already came up with an image of yourself as a gifted marketer. In a sense, you are dressing your online image for the step above where you are currently. You need to appear as someone who wants to take the next step.

Refer to your goal that you previously laid out for your online image. As you look at that goal, what types of steps do you need to take in order to achieve that goal? Is there a stereotype of how you want to present yourself to achieve that goal? Try to find a stereotype that accurately depicts who you want to be. Presenting yourself in this manner signals to everyone that you want to be seen as this type of person.

Don't confuse looking the part with dishonesty. Is it dishonest to dress nicer than you normally would to get a promotion? Absolutely not. You are just playing the game. Conventional wisdom as well as research on the topic indicates people who dress for success often get more promotions. To succeed, you need to show people in the position to promote you that you are capable and able to take the next step. However, if you have decided that your goal is to date the hotties of the world and in order to do so, you have made yourself look like a millionaire when your net worth resides within your piggy bank, your online image is only going to frustrate you and some unsuspecting gold diggers.

Identifying a model person for your future stereotype can help you pick a future stereotype. Imitation is the highest form of flattery, so the saying goes. Obviously if someone is worth imitating they seemingly know what they are doing. Having an idea of what your online image should look like is very useful when you try to create it for the first time. You will want to search the Internet for people you feel have a great online image. People who personify what you want your online image to be are typically leaders in that field. If you are a programmer, try finding leading programmers on the Internet. For instance, if you wanted to be the next visionary programmer, you would look at James Gosling, the inventor of the Java programming language, and see which characteristics he exhibits. Even though he may not have consolidated his image into a single website, you should be able to see articles and biographies outlining his accomplishments. But if you look deeper, you see that he is well educated, ultra-smart, and personifies the ultra-programmer. His accomplishments make sense — they are the trappings of success. Finding the characteristics of these leaders and incorporating them into yours will help you clarify your online image.

At this point, choose your future stereotype. Just like you did when you analyzed your current stereotype, write down the positive and negative characteristics of your future stereotype. When you are finished charting your future stereotype, compare your future stereotype with your current stereotype. Look for gaps between your current stereotype and future stereotype. Circle the areas where you are going to need to improve to reach that stereotype. Put a check mark next to the areas on your future stereotype that matches your current stereotype. These areas will be areas that you can really promote with your online image now. This should give you a clear idea of how you can use the future stereotype as the basis for your online image.

CONSOLIDATING YOUR CURRENT AND FUTURE STEREO-TYPES INTO YOUR ONLINE IMAGE STEREOTYPE

You will need to take your current life stereotype you previously identified and merge it with your future stereotype. Refer to your goal that you previously laid out for your online image. As you look at that goal, what steps do you need to take in order to achieve that goal? Is there a stereotype of how you want to present yourself to achieve that goal? Knowing this information can help you build your online image. Further, if you are able to find someone who has built their online image, you can learn a great deal from how they presented themselves to the world.   You should be able to see how they took a stereo-type and transformed their online image to meet that stereotype.

To see how well you match up with your stereotype, you need to do an assessment of your strengths and weaknesses.   By identify-ing your strengths, you can identify which positive characteristics of a stereotype you can showcase.   By the same token, identification of your weaknesses can help you recognize not to emphasize those aspects of your stereotype.   You will want to write down on the chart your strengths and weaknesses as that type of stereotype.   Consider the case of a computer scientist.   If they are very good at writing code, they should include it as a strength of theirs as a computer program-mer.   Conversely, if they write more bugs than they can fix in the code then that would be a weakness they need to put in the weakness column.

You will want to identify how well you currently stack up against your future stereotype.   If you are having difficulty match-ing up the characteristics to your strengths and weaknesses then you might be missing an important characteristic.   It's OK to modify your stereotype characteristics at anytime if you see the necessity.   If you add characteristics that don't match your stereotype, you may have the wrong stereotype, in which case you may need to re-identify your stereotype.

Review the list of your stereotype characteristics.   Consider how well your strengths match up with the stereotype that you want to portray with your online image.   If you find that the majority of your strengths go to one characteristic, consider the other positive characteristics.   Take a positive characteristic and see if you can iden-tify a new strength that is related to that positive characteristic.

After you consolidate your image, you should now have the stereotype which is the basis for your online image. You will now go through the process of adding additional characteristics specific to the culture you live in.

BEYOND YOUR PERSONAL STEREOTYPE – POSITIVE CHARACTERISTICS FOR QUALITY INDIVIDUALS

In addition to a stereotype, you need to communicate positive characteristics about yourself as a quality individual. For instance, in the United States workplace, most companies emphasize the importance of being a team player. Someone who is a team player is someone who seeks to get along and help the team any way they can. Therefore, being seen as a team player is advantageous for anyone wanting to advance their career. You will want characteristics specific to your culture to be prevalent in your online image.

Most cultures have their own view of what constitutes a quality individual within that culture. A society promotes those people who embody the aspects of their society as cultural heroes within their society. Societies do this to further the goals and perpetuation of an ideal society. In the United States, the qualities of a cultural hero would be characterized as being courteousness, caring, honesty, loyalty, freedom loving, hardworking, and individualistic. An example of a culture promoting cultural heroes, The Boy Scouts of America have captured the quality characteristics of the cultural hero in their Scout Law. The Scout Law states, a Scout is Trustworthy, Loyal, Helpful, Courteous, Kind, Obedient, Cheerful, Thrifty, Brave, Clean and Reverent. All of these characteristics show a quality individual in the American culture.

In other cultures, the characteristics of a quality individual may be completely opposite of the culture you live in. Being seen as a person who embodies the individual your culture sees as a hero will help people see you as the quality individual you are. To complete your online image, you need to incorporate the quality individual characteristics of your culture into your online image.

EXPOSING YOUR LIFE TO THE WORLD

When you build an online image, you need to draw a line in the sand between what constitutes information you are willing to make public and what information you would should keep private. The distinction between public and private information may seem pretty simple, yet people will include information which has no purpose in their online image. As a rule, you should expose areas of your life which promote your goal and nothing else. All you are trying to do is help someone see an aspect of your life as you want them to see that aspect. You are *not* trying to create a resource to help someone be able to learn everything they ever wanted to learn about you.

Some people will want to expose the rest of their family in their online image so that they can use the Internet to showcase their family. While fun to do, the only people that should care about your family connections are other family members and close acquaintances. In other words, a prospective employer has no business checking out pictures of your children.

Your online image should not be a place where you showcase your hobbies unless your goal is to take your hobby prime time. However there is a distinction between showcasing and mentioning hobbies. Mentioning hobbies is fine within an online image because it shows you are interesting and well rounded. However, creating a section of your online image devoted to your hobbies, indicates to the person viewing your online image that you maybe care more about your hobbies than you do your career.

Areas that should be off limits in an online image include your family (especially your children), what you do behind closed doors, your sexual orientation, your religion, your political beliefs, and your relationship history. All of these areas are private and should be treated as private matters. Your children's information should be treated as private.   You wouldn't want a pedophile to be able to use your online image to get information about your children. Other areas of your life you wouldn't want to expose would be to protect yourself from being discriminated against. Employers can't ask you questions about your religion or sexual orientation in an interview, so why would you want to make it easy for them to find that information online?

EXPOSING YOUR SOCIAL NETWORK

When you build your online image you will probably want to expose some members of your social network. Exposing members of your social network can build credibility for your online image which helps address one of the challenges of creating an online image, credibility. The inclusion of reputable individuals within your social network which apply to your online image builds credibility for your online image because of the "birds of a feather flock together concept". Specifically, lawyers should be associating with other lawyers and doctors should be seen with other doctors. People automatically give you more credibility when you look like the stereotype you are professing to be. This is why exposing elements of your social network can be very good for your online image.

Furthermore, some people you may want to include in your online image will help you further your stereotype. To illustrate, let's say that you are a computer scientist. To help your online image, you might want to link to pages from your site to other professional computer scientists you associate with. Linking to their profiles online will make people see you as a well connected computer scientist. Being seen as prominent in your field is never a bad thing for an online image.

Great care should be taken when exposing people who are within your social network. You should always ask yourself, "How is my online image benefitted by the inclusion of their image in mine?" If you are including them in your online image solely on the basis they are your best friend, you should probably leave them off your online image. To include someone in your online image, the person you are including should have a clean online image. If you include someone who has a dirty online image, you may be doing more damage to yourself than the good that you gain from inclusion within your online image.

Moreover, someone may not want you to be tied to them. Don't take it personally if someone doesn't want you to link to them. They are probably managing their online image with this approach as well. As a common courtesy, you should always ask first before linking to a private individual. Chances are people will feel a sense of pride knowing that you want to be associated with them. Furthermore, since you are going to have a great online image, you will be helping them build their online image by including them in yours.

SUMMING IT ALL UP

You should by now be armed with a clear and understandable stereotype that you want to use for your online image. Regardless of your goal, your online image will be a powerful tool in your arsenal to achieve your goal. Used wisely, you will reap the benefits of your online image in several aspects of your life. Because you spent the time to conceive who you are online, you will be able to effectively use your online image for years to come. Onward to building your online image!

CHAPTER EIGHT

BUILD PHASE OF
ONLINE IMAGE MANAGEMENT

*"It takes many good deeds to build a good reputation, and
only one bad one to lose it."*

—Benjamin Franklin, American Founding Father

It's an exciting time for you in the Online Image Management process. You are finally going to see your online image take form. Your efforts to correctly identify your online image stereotype are going to start paying off. In this phase, you will be building the digital equivalent of you on the Internet, your website. This phase will help you to guide the development of your website.

Your role in this process will be that of a project manager with some added duties such as content author and designer. As the project manager of your website build, you should be comfortable with the questions you are going to be asked from your web designer. Your web designer will be responsible for the technical aspects of your website creation.

Let's explore what is involved with getting your website going from start to finish. Here is my recommend approach to building a website for your online image. The build phase is divided into six steps.

The Six Steps of the Build Phase

✓ **Step 1: Get someone to design your website.** — In this step, you will contract with a designer or design company to design your website. You will learn what you need to communicate to a designer to get what you want.

✓ **Step 2: Pick and register your domain name.** — You will determine the appropriate domain name for your online image. You will then register the domain name with a domain name registrar.

✓ **Step 3: Get a company to provide hosting.** — You will learn what you need to know to choose a company to host your website.

✓ **Step 4: Create the structure for your website.** — You will learn how to organize content for your website.

✓ **Step 5: Create the content for your website.** — You will learn what types of content and what to and what not to say on your website.

✓ **Step 6: Evaluating the finished project** — You will learn what you need to do when the designer hands over your website to you.

The progression of the steps should occur in the order I have provided. The build is sequential in its approach and is very similar to building a house. If this were house building, you would take on the role of owner who provides the general ideas about what you want. First of all, you will contract with somebody to build your website which is similar to getting a general contractor who will be handling most of the technical know-how.

If your designer that you are working with prefers proceeding in a different manner for steps 2 – 5 you can deviate from the proscribed order. Just make sure you are getting what you want at the end of the process rather than what the designer wants. Designers have a nasty way of getting what they want since they are the "artists". Let's get started on giving you the information you need to fill the role of the website owner.

BUT I DON'T SPEAK GEEK

The level of technical knowledge required to set up your website might seem daunting at first.   However, with a little help from this book, you could have your own website up and running very quickly.   It really is easier than you might think. Understanding how to build a website can be as technical as you want to make it.   For example, if you look at the earth from space, the earth looks like a blue water ball with clouds and green shaped continents.   At an airline view, about 30,000 ft., you can see features of the landscape, but you can't see the finer details that you see on the ground.   Simply put, as you come closer to the earth, the more detail you can get. In terms of building a website, you will need to know more than the view from space, but you do not necessarily need to know it at a ground level. What you need to know basically is at the airline view.   This means you need to know enough about how a website works to be capable of publishing your own content. Leave the finer details to a web designer.

COSTS INVOLVED

Although not free, costs are relatively miniscule in light of the features and control you will gain by owning your own domain and finding someone to host your site.   Even though ongoing costs may seem steep at first ($5 a month for hosting and $10 a year for domain name registration), you really can't afford not to have your own domain.

Typically, you will end up paying for the design.   The cost can range from $100 on up.   However, don't get caught up in the notion that you need to take out a second mortgage to afford quality design work.   There is not a direct relationship with cost and the quality of a website.   Designers, like most professional services, range greatly in quality.   Some bad designers manage to get paid well and some good ones are cheap and always busy.   What's important for you is to find a designer who is talented and willing to take less than their worth.

OWNING A WEBSITE

Owning your own website can provide you with the same type of joys and frustration similar to owning a home.   Like the pride you feel knowing that you own a piece of the pie and the comfort knowing you have a place that is all your own.   Furthermore, with your own home, you know you are the king or queen of the castle.   On the flip side, there are the taxes to pay, (fees and hosting), seemingly never ending maintenance issues (updating the content, keeping content current), and finding qualified contractors (web designers) to do the work you can't do yourself.   Even with the headaches, website ownership is your best approach to managing your online image.

Like a home, your website says a lot about you. Genetically, we are geared to make snap decisions about who someone is within moments of seeing them. The snap judgments a person might make include the surrounding environment, the quality of the item, and the amount of care given to the item. For example, when you drive up to someone's home you may immediately notice the quality of the neighborhood. You will probably make a rough assessment of the value of the home, and you may notice the car they drive. Furthermore, you can tell whether or not they keep up with the lawn, or the home maintenance. You may even be able to tell what hobbies and other values this person holds dear. All of these characteristics can be ascertained in the first few moments.

Your website carries a first impression that is very similar to that of a home. The first impression a person has, upon visiting your website, will cause the person to form several assumptions about you. Almost immediately, someone will make a snap judgment about the quality of the site and whether or not they like it. They will rate the website based on their limited understanding of personal websites. They will form opinions on the ease of use of your site. They will determine how easy it is to find information on your site.

Like it or not, it will be readily apparent how much time you put into your website. A person could easily infer whether or not you know what you are doing, if you are color-blind or just tasteless. Maybe they'll determine you site is worthless and leave immediately. Based on their assumptions, people will start to choose a stereotype and opinions of you as discussed earlier in the book. Thus, forming a positive first impression is key. The secret to forming a positive first impression is to meet or exceed the visitor's expectation. Remember, your goal should be is to help the visitor form the right stereotype of you.

PAYING ATTENTION TO DETAILS

Similar to a resume, a website can reveal how much effort you spend reviewing and thinking about your bit of cyberspace. It is very important to make the effort to have a quality website. The obvious conclusion a visitor will make, is "If you don't pay attention to detail on your own personal website, how thorough are you going to be on the job?" Conversely, if you impress them with your website, you might land the opportunity you have been seeking. However, to make matters worse, some people impatiently rush to place their website on the Internet. While some people might get away with this approach, most fail miserably because in the rush to get the website out, they often forget about it after it is launched. This approach often leaves an incomplete website at best, and at worst, an absolute mess.

Even more important, once you start directing people to your website, people will start taking a very critical look at your site. It is one thing for a prospective employer to stumble upon your site, while it is quite another to direct them to your site. Advertising a poorly done website is akin to living in the slums and telling people you live in the Hamptons. Especially when you consider the costs of having a professional develop your website can be relatively cheap (under $500) if you shop around for a personal website. A mismanaged website can be a real eye opener to prospective employers if you are trying to market yourself, you will either succeed or fail miserably. However, a professional looking and well written website can be the marketing edge you need to get you in the door.

Your own website provides you with the opportunity to market yourself before, during, and after an information gathering process or interview. Educating the target audience member about who you are helps the target audience member form an understanding of you the way you would like them to see you. By extending the review process you place yourself into higher consideration for potential employment.

If you think of yourself or image as a product that you need to sell, it may be easier to envision your online image. Although, I don't recommend maintaining this approach for the long haul, it may get you started. As a marketing tool, your online image is the best way to put your "best foot forward" in front of a potential buyer. Take a moment to think about the opportunities you have by creating your own website.   The great potential of the opportunity is you control the message and the world is listening. Short of making personal contact or having a network of offline professional contacts, how, in your lifetime, have you had a better opportunity to educate the potential "buyer" of the merits of your "product"? Can't think of any? Neither could I!

The Internet as a marketing medium may be low in terms of in-person contact, but the ability to impress is much higher. You have the ability to craft a message that is unique to you and distribute that message for relatively free.   Furthermore, you can be highly visual in your presentation and provide a multimedia experience that people rarely see on a personal website.

☙ STEP 1 — GET SOMEONE TO DESIGN YOUR WEBSITE ❧

Allow me to introduce you to your new best friend, your web designer. Together you and your designer will build your website. Good chemistry and understanding between a designer and yourself will be important to be able to create the best product possible. (Of course, I am not referring to romantic chemistry. But rather, whether or not you make a good team.)   Pay attention when you select your designer to whether or not you have the chemistry to work together. Talk with them enough before hand to see if you are a good match. You have a vested interest in making your online image look as good as it possibly can. Your designer, at first may only care about the money they are going to make from the project. You need to change their focus from money to helping you. By taking care of your designer, through responding quickly and providing them what they ask for, you can get them invested into the project.   Great teamwork is the result of effective communication. You will need to be able to communicate with your designer and vice-versa. Your designer should be the person who will help you work through all the technical issues.

Building you a web design isn't the designer's only job. They should also be familiar with all elements of building a website.   For instance, the designer should be able to give you their thoughts on reputable companies with whom you may consider hosting your new site.   Additionally, they should be able to explain technical issues to you in a way that you will be able to understand.

Your role will be to tell the designer what you want in clear terms so that each of you understands what the end product should look like.   After all, your online image is the hands of the designer while they build your website.   Being able to describe for them what you want in your online image will help them design a website which satisfies your needs.

WHAT TO LOOK FOR IN A WEB DESIGNER OR DESIGN FIRM

What you should look for in a web designer is someone who can build what you want — a website which reflects your online image. You need someone who can take a stereotype and build that into your website's design.

In order to determine the skill level of the designer, ask for the designer's portfolio. A designer's portfolio should contain samples of the work they have done for other clients. You can learn quite a bit from the portfolio. You should be able to see how detailed they are with their work. To evaluate whether or not they can actually do what you need them to do, look for a key few areas.

EXPERIENCE

Although the design industry is several centuries old, the web design industry is in its infancy. As a profession, web design has been around since 1993. And in the early days, there wasn't much to design until the Internet browser companies built in features which supported colors and other interactive features. So when you look at someone's experience, you are not going to find anyone who can truthfully claim that they have been doing design for thirty years.

Web designers come from a vast array of design experience. Some designers are corporate designers wishing to take on some side projects to supplement income. Other designers are freelance designers by trade and take on projects as they come their way. Still others, work for web design firms.

You should look for a designer or website design firm who has been doing design for more than four years. This gives a designer enough time to have had experience with having to adapt to changing designs. As a design field, fashion plays a key role in design. What is trendy today in design won't be trendy in two years. Having experience with a few trend phases will let you know whether or not a designer can adapt to trends.

If you are selecting a company to work with, the design company should be able to provide you a detailed background of the specific designer you will work with. Ask for that designer's portfolio.

HAVE THEY EVER BUILT WEBSITES FOR AN INDIVIDUAL?

While not a red flag, a designer that has only built websites for companies will sometimes not understand how to present a person. Believe it or not, individuals and companies are different types of entities. As different types of entities, they have different needs as to how to present themselves. A designer that solely focuses on companies may not be able to get the job done when it comes to designing an online image for an individual.

HOW WELL DO THEY CAPTURE THE CONCEPT OF THE SITE?

When you review the website, do you get a good understanding for the purpose of the design. Just by looking at the site without reviewing the content, you should be able to tell how well the designer can communicate with design.   Furthermore, the website design should enhance the product or person. If you feel they haven't been able to capture the product or concept, you'd be better off to go with someone else.

ARE YOU DEALING WITH A FACTORY OR A CUSTOMIZER?

If you are investigating which design firm or designer you are going with you will want to make sure that you are getting the personal attention you need. Some design firms tell their designers they are to spend less than three hours on a client's website design. This includes the time they spend with you on the phone to get an idea of what you want. Of course, the design firm is trying to maximize profits and keep costs low. So it would follow that you and your website are worth less than three hours of their time. For the design of your online image, you need personal attention and more than three hours of a junior designer's time.

DO THEY SHOW DIVERSITY IN DESIGN?

Does the designer build most of their sites from a cookie cutter design? In other words, do the designs look the same from website to website. If the sites look the same, this should be a red flag to you. It can signify that the designer takes a "one size fits all approach" to design. Ultimately, this means that the designer hasn't attempted to understand what they are building, but rather, that the designer has tried to make the website fit their cookie cutter design.

HOW QUICKLY DO THEY RESPOND TO YOU?

The last thing you need is to be in the dark when it comes to your online image. If a pattern of slow response, (longer than a day or two), develops when you are in the first stages of interacting with a designer you should consider this to be a warning of potential inattentiveness to clientele or worse, an overworked designer. Either way, people fall through the cracks and the quality of the design goes down.

DO THEY UNDERSTAND THE CULTURE YOU LIVE IN?

This isn't an attempt to be bigoted or nationalistic. To build an online image website a designer needs to have an understanding of the culture they are designing for.   For instance, if you live in a culture where the color red signifies prostitution and thus communicates you are a streetwalker, you want your designer to know these things natively. The designer needs to understand your culture. You can ascertain this by asking them to describe the stereotype you want to present on the Internet. You should get an answer that incorporates the characteristics you wrote down.

WHAT ARE YOU REALLY GOING TO PAY FOR THEIR SERVICE?

There are two flavors of price scheme that you can expect from a designer when it comes to paying for their services. Some designers will charge an hourly fee while other designers will have a per project bid price. Knowing that a decent designer should be able to do what you want in 8 to 10 hours may help you decide where to go. Either way, you should have an overall estimate of what it is going to cost to have these services provided for you before you commit to anything. The hourly fee developer should be willing to tell you how long it will take them. If they don't know, they should be able to ballpark a figure. However, please note that developers are good at gauging complexity of a project and not so good at gauging time.

While there is no right or wrong way to charge for professional services, you should insist on a cap or limit on whatever pricing scheme the designer and you choose. It is your only protection from having the cost run up on you without your knowledge. For instance, if a designer charges $75 per hour and you don't want the project to exceed $750 put a cap of billable hours at 10 hours unless you authorize more.

You should expect to pay something up-front before a designer is willing to do the work. This often is the case that a designer has done a lot of work for a client, only to have the client dine and dash. Some designers will require a varying percentage of the total fee before they commence work. With any professional service, since you have no collateral if they stiff you and take your money, only pay what you are comfortable paying. If you can't agree on the up front fee, explore other designer options.

Expect that you will be signing a contract which will obligate you. With any contract you should consult professional help before signing your life away.

The following ideas for contract negotiation are only examples and not legal advice.

Contract Negotiation Tips

✓ Ask for a clause that would allow that you receive your deposit back if certain conditions aren't met.

✓ You should be able to ask for a full refund if no work is done on your behalf by an agreed upon date.

✓ Furthermore, you should negotiate a walk clause into the agreement if you and the designer cannot come to an agreement on the site design.

✓ Have the total price and terms of payment included into the contract.

✓ If you are negotiating an hourly cost, build into the contract that you can get a report of what work was done per hour.

✓ Include the maximum cap of what you are willing to pay.

FINDING THE DESIGNER

A simple place to look for a web designer is of course, the Internet or your local yellow pages directory. There are also several freelance websites where designers will bid on projects. Searching your favorite search engine for "web design" should return more choices than you will know what to do with.   If you want to narrow that down, you can search by various terms such as the state or city you live in along with the term web designer. The search results should direct you to the respective web designer's website. By looking at their website, you should be able to view their online portfolio, or at the very least some examples of their work. Look for people who can design a great looking website. A great looking website is clean and draws your eyes to the important elements of the page, such as the content.

You should pick the three top designers that you think can build an online image for you. You will need to contact each of them and request a quote for their services. Expect to have to explain to them what you are trying to do and spend a bit of time with each of them, probably over the phone.

Always ask for their client references. References will tell you more about how the designer works with clients. You need to know if the reference encountered problems such as resistance to design changes or maintenance nightmares. It would also be great for you to know how accurate the bid was. Finding out whether or not they experienced unanticipated costs would be really good to know. Ask the reference if they feel like the designer captured the essence of the product quickly or if they needed frequent correction.

COMMUNICATING THE REQUIREMENTS OF YOUR WEBSITE

Your designer is the expert when it comes to the technical aspect of development. But you are the expert in getting what you want out of an online image. It will be important for you to communicate with the designer. You will need to explain to the designer what you are trying to do with your online image. Your charted stereotype from the previous section should help a designer know what you are looking for in a website. You have already done the hard work in identifying what your online image should communicate. Share with your designer the characteristics that you want your online image to reflect. If they haven't helped someone build an online image before they will need to get a basic understanding of the overall approach to presenting a stereotyped version of you.

Help the designer understand your goal for your online image. Communicating with them this goal makes what you are doing a team effort. Generally speaking, people want to help each other. We feel good about ourselves when we help out our fellow man. If the designer understands your goal, you will have moved your relationship towards creation of a great Online Image Management team.

By communicating the requirements of your website to your designer, you should be able to get a feel for whether or not they have built sites like this before. If what you throw at them doesn't seem to faze them, ask for example sites which you can see similar components in action. If the designer has never built a site like this, you may need to find an alternate designer. You certainly do not want to pay for them to learn on your dime. Talk to the designer about what kind of content you anticipate putting out there. Tell them you will want four to five categories for content and at the most ten to fifteen pages of content.

ABILITY TO PASSWORD PROTECT PARTS OF YOUR WEBSITE

While the majority of your website should be accessible to everyone, some of the website you may want to have password protected. This password protection doesn't need SSL (basically encrypted for security- you won't need to do this unless you're doing e-commerce transactions on your page) but you want to keep people who shouldn't access content from getting to the protected content. A password can be given to those you want to have access to the information a prospective employer given access to your online resume or you mother access to pictures of you and your dog. It may be nice if you could give user ID's for tracking purposes, but you shouldn't be willing to pay much extra for that capability.

A TOOL TO DO THE MAINTENANCE YOURSELF

Tell your designer you will want the ability to do maintenance yourself. Basically, you need a website that you will be able to update and manage after they have moved on to other projects. You should explain that you would prefer if there was a built in, password protected tool to do editing with. A What You See Is What You Get (WYSIWYG pronounced Wiz-E-Wig) editing tool which you can update the site with. You don't want them to build a tool for you, only that you want a commercially available free or cheap tool.

A BLOG

You want a blogging tool installed on your website, preferably Wordpress or something in the same category. Your blog should have a very similar look and feel as your website. In other words, the transition between your blog and your website should be relatively seamless.

SITE STATISTICS SOFTWARE

Site statistics software is your window into how people use your website. You will be able to see where people are visiting your site from. Further, you will be able to see what pages they look at and what search terms brought them to your site.

THE DESIGN PROCESS

Before you contract with a designer, ask them to detail the design process they use to you so you have an understanding of what they want to do and how they plan to go about doing it. Pay attention to how often they involve you in the design process. Avoid a designer that only involves you to get an idea of what you want and the next time you hear from them is at the tail end of the process. If you are only consulted at the very beginning and again at the end of design, you haven't been given the opportunity to be an influence your website's design.

The designer you are working with should have a process to find out what you want in a design. A good designer will attempt to understand what you want to do in order to assess what you need technology wise. Typically, a designer will ask you for example website designs you like. They do this so they can know how to design what you are looking for. While this is OK for the designer to do, sometimes they will end up building what you like and not necessarily the stereotype that you want them to build into your design. If you get asked this question, don't shoot from the hip. Have some sample sites ready to give out upon request.

Typically, the designer will go off and build a few designs or comps for you to choose from before they make you commit to a particular design. You should be able to tell them what you like and what you don't. An experienced designer won't hold it against you if you don't like their design. They may try to explain why they went a certain direction. If you agree with them, you can go with what they have done.

Once you commit to the design, the designer will help you determine how people are going to get to your website. The designer should have experience in dealing with domain registration and domain hosting. They should be able to give you ideas of who to go with and what features you are going to need. When you have the details of what domain name you are planning on using and which hosting company you are going to use, the designer will move on to building your website. The designer will ask you for pictures that they may be able to incorporate into the design of your website. If the designer doesn't ask for this, request that they incorporate pictures of you into your design.   The pictures you will want to include will depend of the stereotype you are trying to present. For example, if you are a high school student trying to get into a select university, you may want pictures of you volunteering and participating in your appropriate extracurricular activities.

Depending on the designer, they may contact you while they build the skeleton of your website, but most likely they will contact you once the skeleton is complete. For many designers, they will build the template for the site and then whenever they create a new page will use the template.

While the designer is busy building the skeleton of your site, the designer will want you to write the content for the website and help with organizing the content on your website. You will usually agree upon a time frame where you are going to provide the text, also known as content. Although organization (menu structure) will be something that the designer will try to get from you ASAP, as it is part of the design. If you need more time, don't be afraid to ask for it. The designer can use generic categories and generic content until you have what the structure the way you want it.

Once you hand the content over, the designer will take the content and place it into the skeletal structure. The designer will then contact you and ask you to review the site structure. Take the opportunity to be nitpicky. After this final revision step any major changes to the website are going to cost you.

One final step which is often overlooked by designers is maintenance of the website of which you are the proud owner. If you have negotiated the ability to maintain your website, you should receive training on how to update your website. Text changes and layout within the content portion of the webpage are areas where you should be able to update by yourself without incurring additional charges.

❧ STEP 2 — PICK AND REGISTER YOUR DOMAIN NAME ❦

Choosing the right domain name is a pretty important decision when it comes to Online Image Management. Search engines key off the terms they find in a URL when they determine how likely it is this website contains the information contained within the search request. You will need to acquire a domain name that has your name contained within it for maximum effectiveness.

BUYING A DOMAIN - HOW TO

There are two main approaches to purchasing your domain name. The first way is to purchase your domain name, design, and hosting bundled as a package. The second way is to purchase them separately. Both approaches have pros and cons. The decision will be up to you to decide which way you want to go.

THE BUNDLED APPROACH

The bundled approach has some distinct advantages. It can be summed up as the one stop shopping experience. This means you will manage all aspects of your site with one company. You may get a package deal as well. If you go with the bundled approach, make certain you do your homework. Unfortunately, the more services you bundle, the less ability you will have to choose the best provider for the service you want. Essentially, you will not have the opportunity to select the best hosting company and the best design firm, or the best domain registration company. With bundling, you may get a company that does one of the aforementioned services well, but little else. If you chose a firm that focuses on web design and development, you should expect them to only be experts in their area of expertise.

If you choose to bundle services you may encounter a potential headache. If you ever become dissatisfied with the service, changing providers can be quite difficult. Because the company registers your domain name, you may have to deal with them to release the control of your domain name. This depends on how they set up the contacts for your domain name. If they list themselves as the administrative and technical contact, proving ownership to a domain name registrar will be difficult.

Another reason it can also be difficult to switch, is because you have to go through customer retention sorts of maneuvers from the hosting provider. If you have ever closed a credit card account, you most likely understand the pain and torment of telling someone no repeatedly.

BUYING DOMAIN HOSTING AND DOMAIN NAME REGISTRATION SEPARATELY

Purchasing these two products separately will give you more flexibility to change the companies you use for domain hosting and domain registration. Since you have complete control over both aspects of your website hosting, you can leverage the ability to switch providers while getting the best of breed. (I prefer to purchase these separately because I like the control I enjoy over my domain name without having to deal with the company I purchase hosting from.)

There are several companies that give you the ability to purchase your own domain name. When it comes to domain name registration, there are several good companies to choose from. Most offer some variation of their service, but ultimately they all offer the same product: registration of your domain name. Since you are choosing to do domain name registration through a company, you don't need any other service than domain name registration from them.

One choice you will have when registering a domain name will be to add a privacy feature. The privacy feature masks your information from the publicly available registry of domain owners. It's the equivalent of having your phone number privately listed. Although some people like to add the privacy feature, that is up to you. In this manner, no one will be able to easily look at who is the owner of your website.

The key search term for this type of company is "domain name registration". You may see companies like Godaddy or Network Solutions in your search results. These companies are technically called registrars. All of these companies provide similar services. The main considerations you should use are price and reputation. Price is a good consideration to use because that is an easy comparison when there is very little difference between companies.

GO WITH A NAME BRAND REGISTRAR.

I highly recommend going with one of the big companies when you choose who to register your domain name with. Smaller registrars are often reselling the services of the larger companies. Why would you want to pay the middle man, when you will end up using the rebranded product of the original company anyway? Consult with your web designer as to which of these companies you should go with. Their experience with various registrars will be useful to you if you choose to unbundle the domain name registration from domain hosting.

CHOOSING THE RIGHT DOMAIN NAME

Once you have found the company you want to register your domain name with, then the hard part comes, choosing your domain name. You will need to choose the domain name as well as the appropriate extension. For the sake of attracting the people looking for you to your website, the domain name you choose needs to have your name in it. This gives the information seeker, at a minimum, the feedback that they have found someone who shares your name. Furthermore, when your name is searched for, search engines will be able to place your website higher in those search results.

Choosing the right domain name can be quite fun and quite frustrating all at the same time. The fun part, is seeing your name in lights. There is something special about the opportunity to own your very own domain name. The frustrating part, will most likely be choosing a domain name, depending on the uniqueness of your full name.

The process of finding a domain name that isn't registered can be an exercise in futility. However, if you are flexible with your domain name, a little bit of trial-and-error can do wonders. If at first you don't succeed in finding your domain name and extension (e.g., mywebsite.com), you will need to make variations to your spelling of the domain name or accept subpar extensions if you must have the yourname.whatever.

WHAT SHOULD MY DOMAIN NAME BE

Before we begin picking a domain name there are a few considerations we need to use. Review the six general guidelines.

Six General Guidelines for Picking Great Domain Names

✓ **Less is more.** The shorter a domain name the better. Using a short domain name is preferred because it's easier to remember and it lessens the likelihood of misspellings.

✓ **Domain names run words together.** By convention, it is widespread practice to run words/names together in a domain name. This works OK most of the time. Sometimes you can get other words that are created by accident.

✓ **Domain names can only use certain characters.** You are limited to letters a through z (case-insensitive), digits 0 through 9, and hyphens.

✓ **Connect the domain name to you.** Someone who hardly knows you should be able to draw a strong connection between you and your website based on URL alone. Your name should be part of the Domain name.

✓ **Readability is Key.** The URL should be readable by the average person. Sometimes names when put together don't flow the way the owner originally intended. Case in point, take someone named Wilma Armana. If she registered her first and last name as a domain name, the domain name would look like wilmaarmana.com. Capitalizing letters of the name would help if you control how someone reads your domain name (WilmaArmana.com), however, hyphenating the name would be the better choice.(Wilma-Armana.com)

✓ **The domain name should avoid unintended misreading.** For example, my favorite domain name to illustrate this point has always been experts-exchange.com. Notice the unintended misreading if you drop the hyphen.

For the purposes of illustrating the thought process for picking a domain name for your site, let's assume we are helping John Jacob Jingleheimer-Schmitt (insert your obvious joke here) pick a website domain name.   John, like you, wants to create a website to control his online image.   John needs to decide the domain name for his website. John should begin by creating a list consisting of a top domain names he would like to use. As possible choices for the domain URL are added to the list, John should put them into the proper URL format (http://www.example.com). This way John can see immediately how it will look. He can evaluate the domain name based on the criteria listed above.

The first entry on to the list should be his name that he goes by commonly.   In this case we will assume that he goes by John Schmitt. His first entries on the list should include his first and last name as first choice to acquire johnschmitt.com, johnschmitt.net. If John is known to the world as Jake Schmitt, and John doesn't use his full name, jakeschmitt.com makes much more sense. People who know John as Jake will search for "Jake Schmitt" and not "John Schmitt".

Now, John should take into account how he uses his name in professional settings. The most likely place to look at how he uses his name professionally is on his resume. If John goes by his full name on his resume, he should use that within his domain name, http://www. johnjacobjingleheimerschmitt.com. This domain name makes sense from the standpoint that it is the name he uses to present himself professionally to the world. Secondly, if he uses his full name, people will validate the page as authentic in their minds. Lastly, the domain name would be appropriate for use in a resume and helps attract top search results when employers search for information about John.

John should then consider the difficulty of spelling his name accurately. Since there are quite a few people who can spell John Jacob Jingleheimher-Schmitt,(the song is still running through my head) this shouldn't be a problem for John. However, if you are one of the lucky few that have a name that is difficult to spell, you can come up with common variations to a domain name. In John's situation, he may choose to register a domain based on a variation of a longer domain name. http://www.J3Schmitt.com/ might be easier to tell someone over the phone than http://www.johnjacobjingleheimerschmitt.com.

Next John should consider how unique his name is.   Since

John's name, all joking aside, is quite unique, John shouldn't have a problem getting the domain name he wants.   However, if his name were John Smith it would be difficult to acquire any domain name using a standard approach.   John would need to read the upcoming section on variations to come up with ideas to get a great domain name.

A COMMON NAME: VARIATIONS AND TECHNIQUES TO GET A GREAT DOMAIN NAME

Chances are your name is not unique.   In my case, because my name is fairly unique, I was easily able to register aaronfrancesconi.com.   Lucky for me, none of the other three Aaron Francesconi's of the world have bothered before I did to register aaronfrancesconi.com.

To illustrate how someone with a common name could find a great domain name, let's use an alternate persona named John Smith.   While the most obvious choice for John would be to register johnsmith.com.   While it is not probable that johnsmith.com is available for registration, it is always worth a try.   It is a trap to always think that domain names are always registered.

Pay attention to what you are trying to convey.   In general, avoid using nicknames because they tend to convey additional meaning.   If I told you my nickname in high school which has stuck with me throughout all these years, your stereotype of me would change almost instantly.   Don't believe me? It's SconeDawg. Now, you are thinking, maybe he likes delicious scones a bit too much, or he was given the nickname when everyone in the world appended "Dawg" to their nickname.   Either way, nicknames are very specialized to you and those around you.   Outsiders won't get the meaning of your nickname without explaining it to them.   Once again, avoid using nicknames in your domain name.

There is one exception to this rule. John might go by JJ Smith. Use of a nickname is appropriate when you use your nickname as your real name. In this case, jjsmith.com would be very appropriate. If your nickname is "the hammer", it may be considered inappropriate www.jjthehammersmith.com or jjthehammer.com because it could give the wrong impression and form the wrong stereotype.   Do you really want them thinking that you are into the Olympic sport of hammer throwing, carpentry or perhaps that you are in to 80's television reruns?

Some quick and easy variations of a domain name

- **Hyphenating your name:** john-smith.com

- **Using your middle name:** JohnJacobSmith.com

- **Appending your zip code:** JohnSmith90210.com

- **Appending your city, state:** JohnSmith-of-Nevada.com

- **Being declarative:** I-am-JohnSmith.com

- **Using statements:** JohnSmithForHire.com

- **Declaring your profession:** JohnSmith-guitarist.com

WHY THE .EXTENSION MATTERS

The last part of a URL or a domain name is the known as the TLD (top level domain) or extension. The general TLDs in use worldwide are .com, .net, and .org. Most people are familiar with URL's ending in one of these three generic extensions. Although the original intent was for people to use the appropriate extensions, people quickly learned the value of using a .com domain name for most purposes.

Because of the explosive use of the internet, the agency which oversees the registration of these domain names responded by adding more TLDs. These TLDs vary in familiarity. Although at last count, there were 281 TLDs, how many can you think of? Not 281, that's for sure. Some companies have become very creative in the use of domain name and the 281 available extensions. The social bookmarking website, http://del.icio.us is one of the more creative uses of a domain name. Notice that del.icio.us is a complete URL and it cleverly spells the word delicious. (Now that's easy to remember) Using the domain name, icio and extension .us, combined with del (which is the equivalent of using the conventional www) the company is able to make the .us extension really work for them.

You can try to be clever with the domain name and extension combination, if your name allows. However, I would remind you that search engines will not be able to fully associate the URL with you. For example, someone name John Abericous might be able to register john.Aberico.us and have the domain john.Aberico.us. To a search engine, this will appear as John Aberico. It will make it difficult for people to find the official John Abericous website.

For your purposes, when making a choice of TLD and extension, use .com, .net, .name, and .org in that order or priority. The TLDs are common enough to be easily remembered and not considered strange by the general public.

TRIAL AND ERROR – THE ONLY WAY TO GET A DOMAIN NAME

The best practice for determining if a domain name is available is to visit a domain name registration (registrar) company's website, and check to see if the domain name is available. Typically on the homepage of the company you choose, there will be a place for you to perform a domain name search. Often, the webpage will only ask you for the domain name and not the extension.

When you search for the domain name you would like, the domain registrar returns results which show whether or not it is available. Most of these registrars will show other possible combinations of your domain name with alternate extensions. For instance, you searched for jingleheimerschmitt.com and found it wasn't available. However, jingleheimerschitt.net is available for registration.

If you find the domain you want is available for registration, you can quickly register it and be done with the entire process. Alternatively, if the domain name you seek is not available, you will be given other options. Sometimes these alternate computer generated choices can be some remarkably good URLs. It will definitely be worth your time to review alternate options that were returned by the registrar.

Additionally, many registrars show you your domain name with various extensions (TLDs) combinations. Instead of the .com extension you wanted, you may be able to get the .net or .org extension. If you do not like the alternate options, you can try to vary your original domain names with slight variations to get the domain name you want.

BEFORE YOU REGISTER YOUR DOMAIN NAME

There is one final check to do before you register a domain name. You need to check out the history and footprint of the domain name before you register it. Domain names tend to change hands from time to time. Some people often use domain names for a purpose that never really pans out. So once they are done with their Internet experiment, they often let the domain name go. You will want to make sure that the site has a clean bill of health and hasn't been used for things like porn.

Search engines take snapshots of your website as they visit

them.   Searching for a domain name can tell you which people still have links to the website.   From these links you should be able to ascertain what the website was used for and how popular it was.

A great way to check out the history of a website is use the Internet archive http://www.archive.org/.   You can see the history of your would-be domain name.   Once you take ownership of the domain, you will want to request from the Internet archive that you do not want to be included in the archive anymore. (In case, you need to change your stereotype a few times in the future.)

BUT I REALLY WANT MYNAME.COM

It is not a foregone conclusion that if a domain name is already registered that you would be unable to acquire the domain name.   But before you get your heart set on purchasing Ihavetohavemyname.com, remember that the strategy is to help search engines find you, and for people to be able to associate the domain name with you.   John-smith.com might be available and would accomplish the goals of registering an appropriate domain name for the domain name strategy.

If you insist on owning a johnsmith.com -like domain, there are several potential events that could free up a registered domain name.   The events range from the domain expiring to the domain owner releasing the domain registration to a domain having its ownership transferred.   The quickest way to acquire the domain name you want from someone else, would be to offer to purchase the registered domain name from the owner of the domain name.   The price you pay will be a function of demand and determination of the owner to hold on to the website.   While the supply of a domain names is potentially unlimited, the owner knows that you want their domain name, which limits your negotiating power.

Before contacting the owner of the website, you will need to do some homework beforehand.   This is a very important step to determine if you even want the domain name.   First and foremost, you need to see if the domain name is being used.   This is simply done by visiting johnsmith.com.   If it is obvious that the domain is being used by John Smith, you will probably need to offer more money to get John Smith to transfer ownership of his domain name.

Secondly, make certain that he has not littered the Internet with garbage about himself on his website.   Do a profile of his website using the techniques described in earlier chapters of this book.   If you find there is too much out there to make it worth owning johnsmith. com then stop worrying about it and be glad that you can distinguish yourself from him. Lastly, is the owner of the website famous or a historical figure like John Smith?   If so, you might want to reconsider purchasing the domain name. They may not be willing to give it up.

Based on the homework above, determine what you are willing pay for the domain name.   Keep in mind that your best alternative to acquiring this domain name is to register one that isn't registered for $10. Ask yourself, "If you owned the domain name, what would you be willing to sell the domain name for?" Maybe $100 or $1,000,000 is appropriate to acquire the domain name. It all comes down to whether or not you are willing to pay the money necessary. Nevertheless, I recommend setting a price you are willing to pay that you wouldn't have buyer's remorse if you were to acquire the domain name.

Although this might take more time than you would like, you may be able to wait out the person who has registered the domain name.   If you recall, domains are registered for a set time period (typically in years).   At some point if someone forgets to pay the annual fees for the domain name, purposefully does not renew, or perhaps they have, heaven forbid, died, the domain name will become available for registration again.   Once the domain name is available, you can try to grab it before someone else does.

If you want an automated solution, backordering the domain or contracting with a company that specializes in drop catching services may be the way to go.   The strategies involved with acquiring a domain in this manner are beyond the scope of this book. If you want to learn more, search the Internet for "Backorder domain".

✥ STEP 3 — GET A COMPANY TO PROVIDE HOSTING ✥

You are faced with several options for hosting.   Some of the options available to you are free, but don't get too excited. All of the free solutions are not ideal because you have to give up freedom in order to get their service.   For example, in exchange for free website space, these companies by placing advertisements on and around your content.   The problem this approach presents multiple concerns. 1) You do not control the advertisements on our site, so you can't be sure if they are appropriate.   2) You do not control the placement of these ads which takes away valuable real estate on your website.   3) The URL that you are given is controlled by the company. For example, http:// geocities.yahoo.com/userabc/ is not exactly a friendly web URL to put on your resume nor is it search engine optimized.

Typically, an Internet account offered by your Internet Service Provider (ISP) comes with a bit of storage space (http://aaronf123. freeAdForMyISP.com/), an e-mail account (aaron@ freeAdForMyISP. com), and Internet access.   However, what you are doing is providing your ISP with a free advertisement every time you use their e-mail or hosting.   It's a free ad, because their domain URL is part of your e-mail address and website URL.   Anyone who wants to visit your site or send you an e-mail has to enter their domain name.

Even though it is not ideal, using your ISP for free website hosting isn't a horrible approach. It is free and it could be a good way to get your feet wet with website building. However, you will use their service at your own peril and you miss an important marketing opportunity. But since the costs are so low, I would only recommend this approach if you are penniless.

And then there are the social networking websites. Several of the options for hosting content are en vogue at the moment with your peers, like MySpace and Facebook. While some of these social network sites are fairly easy to use, well liked by your peers, and for the most part free, they too have advertisements on and around your content. Furthermore, some of these sites may carry with them a stigma associated with the site. For example, MySpace is considered by many, a website for teenagers and having a MySpace page for a 50 year old executive doesn't quite fit the mold.

What you need in a home for your content is complete control of the look and feel of your website. In addition, you need to be able to change content quickly, and drive search engines in droves to your message on the Internet. What you need is your own domain name and website hosting.

WHAT TO LOOK FOR IN A WEBSITE HOSTING COMPANY

Like sand on a seashore, there is a seemingly endless supply of web hosting companies. All of the web hosting companies offer the same basic service, providing a home for your website. Where they differ is how they provide the web hosting. Without getting too technical, the type of hosting they provide depends on what type of web development platform they are trying to support. The web development platform requires four components, the operating system which everything runs on, the web server which serves up the website to your browser, the database which stores data for your website, and the language a developer can use to write data-driven web pages. A common model for hosting companies to use for their cheapest package is to bundle the free, open source software to provide a web development platform for your web designer. This is often referred to as the LAMP platform (**L**inux - the operating system, **A**pache – the webserver, **M**ySql – the database, **P**HP –the scripting language). Thanks to heavy competition and the free software, hosting packages that use the LAMP platform run in the $6 to $15 per month range. Based on the requirements for your website, the LAMP platform should meet your needs.

Your web designer may want to use a different platform, (Java, .NET, (pronounced Dot Net)) to give you the capabilities you asked for. If this is the case, make sure you don't end up paying a premium because the designer is comfortable with a different platform and doesn't want to have to learn a new technology.

You can allow the designer to build the site with a different platform, as long as you are OK with the probable higher cost of hosting. However, you need to realize that when a web hosting provider offers one of the other web development platforms their costs go up. The other platforms typically involve technology which needs to be paid for and licensed from a company. As such, web hosting companies have to pass this cost on to you. So be prepared to have to pay more money on a monthly basis for hosting if you allow the designer to build a solution with a different platform.

After the web development platform decision, there is even a more dizzying amount of options to choose from. What's important to you is the capabilities of the server from the standpoint of what you need.

E-MAIL ACCOUNTS AND ACCESS

Often the amount of e-mail addresses you can have is an option which will distinguish packages. You shouldn't need many e-mail addresses. After all, many people won't want to use theirname@ yourdomainname.com for their e-mail address. Having the option for web based e-mail is a nice feature you should look for. Although not important for Online Image Management, it is a nicety that you should be able to have installed on your account.

MULTIPLE DOMAINS

Often the hosting company will let you host multiple domain names under the same account for the same price as it would be for one. This is a nice option to split the cost of hosting with no down-side to you. Multiple members of your immediate family can share the space and bandwidth. If the hosting company lets you host multiple domains under the same account, you should pick this option.

THE SPACE REQUIREMENTS

You will most likely have minimal space requirements. You won't need more than their base package unless you're planning on doing something really fancy.

THE BANDWIDTH REQUIREMENTS

To start with, you won't need to purchase any package that gives you a lot of bandwidth. The minimal package should be all you need for Online Image Management.

THE MONTHLY TRANSFER REQUIREMENTS

Unless you have some reason that you are going to get an awful lot of traffic on your website, a minimal package should meet your needs.

Your web designer should be able to help with the hosting provider decision. Don't agonize over this decision. Most hosting companies will be just fine for your needs. Like all things, do your homework before you buy and you will be just fine.

&STEP 4 — CREATE THE STRUCTURE FOR YOUR WEBSITE &

The purpose of structure is to organize your content in an easy to sort through manner. Seemingly, it may be difficult to categorize your nonexistent content, while at the same time, without the structure, you won't know where your hodgepodge of data is supposed to go. For our purposes, we will start out by creating the structure. The structure will give you the plan for what to put on your online image. That way you will have a great idea where to begin when you start writing content for your website.

In general, websites need to be able to provide you with information on the subject they are presenting. Often this is done by giving you a choice of categories you can read about. These categories constitute the menu structure for the website. Visit a few websites to see how they categorize their content. You will notice how a category intuitively communicates the information in that section.

Selecting categories to include is where your online image stereotype will help you immensely. While there are a few default categories I am going to recommend, you will want to tailor the categories to meet your stereotype. For instance, for a computer programmer, a sample structure would be "About Me, Computer Programming, My Blog, For Prospective Employers, My Portfolio".

To start with, you will want to select four to five categories. Of course, you could start out with more or less but 4 to 5 categories seem to be sufficient for an online image. In the future, you can always add or remove categories if you need them. What you need to think about as you add categories is what your stereotype would find important enough to be able to write on several topics in that category. So for a prospective college student, they may see a need to write about their friends (only showing friends that help their image), the extracurricular activities, organizations they belong to, and awards they have been awarded. The categories you choose will help form a first impression of what interests you while solidifying your online image.

RECOMMENDED CATEGORIES FOR EVERYONE

ABOUT ME

An about me category gives you the opportunity to educate the person about who you are. The about me category is something that is expected when a visitor arrives at your website. This category has a giant bulls eye on it in terms of interest. Everyone wants to find out who they are learning about. Most people will want to read this section. The about me category is a great place to tell your story. Telling your story is a great way to communicate on the personal level. This is an area where you can selectively show yourself as an individual.

MY BLOG

A blog is an excellent place to solidify your online image in the mind of the website visitor. This is a category that will show off what you are interested in like no other.   More importantly, the blog is a place where your stereotype can show what they are interested in.

TARGETED AUDIENCE

Targeted audience members will naturally be drawn to this section. If employment is your target, you should name this category, "For Potential Employers." The section is appealing to them, because it is created for them. After all, it has their name written all over it. This category will give resources for your targeted audience.

By providing a category for your targeted audience, you are sending a clear message to the website visitors, which is, go here. As you learned earlier, a clear online image is vital to effective communication. If you were applying for a job, directing your targeted audience to this portion of your website gives you the opportunity to put additional content like an expanded resume with examples, charts and graphs, pictures. Imagine what possibilities exist with a medium as great as the Internet.

CATEGORIES BASED ON YOUR STEREOTYPE'S INTERESTS

You should have one or two categories that reflect the interests of your stereotype. These categories should be reflective of what your stereotype would write on the web if it could. For example, an accountant would have a section on accounting. An executive could have sections on leadership or corporate responsibility. In this category, the executive could showcase examples of them providing leadership.

The goal for each category you create is to be able to exemplify most, if not all of the characteristics of your stereotype. As you identify the categories you want to include on your personal website, think about how this category is broad enough that I can include three to five topics underneath this category. Further, think about what types of materials you could put in the category you are considering. For instance, if I am a high school student hoping to get into a selective college, creating a "For Admission Committee" would be a great category, because I could supplement my application for the university. I could add video, stories, and or multimedia presentations which shows me exemplifying the characteristics I believe they are looking for all within the same category.

TOPICS

After you outline the categories your website will have, you should create the topics underneath each category. Topics should be a specific segment of a category. For instance, in your "About Me" category, you should have topics such as "My Story", "My Goals", and "My Interests". These topic labels can be changed to something which more reflects you. The intent of these topics is to show you what types of information you can include when it comes to topics underneath the "About Me" category. To identify topics for each category you are going to want to consider how you can bring out the characteristics of your stereotype.

Topics should be supportive of the category they are in. It should be obvious to the website visitor, why that topic is included underneath that category. This approach will help build the strength of each category as reflective of who you are. For instance, if you had a category about "Student Activities", you should see topics that would be student activities. A topic like, "Conflict between Israel and the Muslim world" may only fit if you were an activist at your school for that particular cause. Even then, mentioning that topic adds a political element to your online image which is something you may want to stay away from. If you add politics to your image, someone may discriminate against you. (Of course, you can have political messages on your website if you are a politician and your online image's goal is to support your political aspirations.)

Aim for three to five topics per category. A good rule of thumb is, if you can't get at least two topics for a category, then you don't have enough topics and should consider consolidating your category with another category. On the flip side, when you are starting out, if you added more than 5 topics per category, you will have to expand the website to the point that you run the risk of too much information. Further, as you build more content into your online image, you add time that you will need to maintain that additional content.

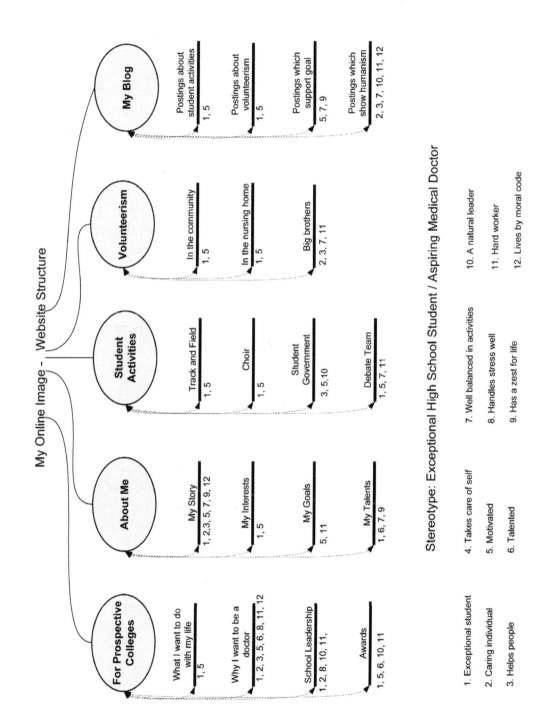

My Online Image - Website Structure

For Prospective Colleges
- What I want to do with my life — 1, 5
- Why I want to be a doctor — 1, 2, 3, 5, 6, 8, 11, 12
- School Leadership — 1, 2, 8, 10, 11,
- Awards — 1, 5, 6, 10, 11

About Me
- My Story — 1, 2, 3, 5, 7, 9, 12
- My Interests — 1, 5
- My Goals — 5, 11
- My Talents — 1, 6, 7, 9

Student Activities
- Track and Field — 1, 5
- Choir — 1, 5
- Student Government — 3, 5, 10
- Debate Team — 1, 5, 7, 11

Volunteerism
- In the community — 1, 5
- In the nursing home — 1, 5
- Big brothers — 2, 3, 7, 11

My Blog
- Postings about student activities — 1, 5
- Postings about volunteerism — 1, 5
- Postings which support goal — 5, 7, 9
- Postings which show humanism — 2, 3, 7, 10, 11, 12

Stereotype: Exceptional High School Student / Aspiring Medical Doctor

1. Exceptional student
2. Caring individual
3. Helps people
4. Takes care of self
5. Motivated
6. Talented
7. Well balanced in activities
8. Handles stress well
9. Has a zest for life
10. A natural leader
11. Hard worker
12. Lives by moral code

CHARTING THE STRUCTURE OF YOUR WEBSITE

Having a visual representation of what your website should be structured like will help you understand the interrelation between your categories and your topics. Through this understanding, you can take it a step further by identifying major stereotype characteristics for each topic. This will add clarity and guide you as you begin the process of creating content for each of the topics. Referring to the charted website structure on the prior page, you will see a completed structure. Notice how the topics are underneath the category that the topic applies to. Further, each topic has the corresponding characteristics which are to be emphasized for that topic.

First, identify the categories you want your online image website to have. The recommended categories, "About me" and "My Blog" should be added under the label that you want them to appear. Next, add the one to two categories on the stereotype interest. Finally, add your targeted audience. Identify the topics you want your online image to have.

You should add the four recommended topics underneath the about me category. These topics are "My Story", "My Goals", "My Interests", and "My Inspiration". If you feel as if you want to change the topic label, so that you don't appear like two million other websites, feel free to make changes to the label. Just know that the idea behind those topics should be addressed somehow. Write down the remaining topics as they relate to each of the categories. Remember to try for three to five topics per category.

Identify which stereotype characteristics you want to showcase in each of the topics. Copy the characteristics you want to portray in your online image into your website structure chart. Write the corresponding number of the characteristic underneath each of the topic that you want to emphasize within that topic.

❧ STEP 5 — CREATE THE CONTENT FOR YOUR WEBSITE ❧

Without content, you have no message. In the land of the Internet, content is King. Content refers to the material within each of the topics. Content can come in many forms. From video to text, pictures to sound clips — if you can make it digital, you can turn it into content. Ultimately, content is what helps you and what hurts you. Content that is well constructed improves your online image. In contrast, content that is poorly constructed hurts your online image.

Using image conscious content transforms a website into your online image. Content is the part of the website build that your designer can't help you that much. Web designers are good at what they do, (and while some of them can do more than just write code for a webpage) writing is not what they do best. Web designers are web designers for a reason. If they enjoyed writing, they would have become English majors, and went on to become an editor. Besides, would you really want to trust your online image to someone who has more fun with pixels more than they do a person. (There I go perpetuating a stereotype, again).

The content you include on your online image will be derived from the structure you developed for your online image. The structure you created will keep you focused from creating content that has no place on your website. Each topic will have a text write up to help communicate the message.

WHAT CAN YOU DO WITH CONTENT

Content is where you have the ability to shine and distinguish yourself from six billion people. Content can be creative, fun and online image friendly all at the same time. You no longer have to think in black, white, and plain.   It's like going from a box of crayons with 6 colors and going to the 128 color crayon box complete with crayon sharpener.   Your options of what you can do are only bound by imagination and creativity.

Multimedia content on the Internet gives you the ability to communicate better than you could if all you had were written words. While writing is a good form of communication, it is limited because you can only communicate with words. Communication is more than words, in our day to day interaction with other humans most of our communication is nonverbal. That is, how you look at somebody while they are talking to you to how you hold your hands, all communicates.

The Internet gives you the ability to take multiple forms of singular media content and combine them to create multi-media content. For instance, if I were to write about my favorite place along the Oregon coast and describe it in vivid detail, you would get a good feel for what I was describing.   I could tell you about the rocky beach were the grey mist that seems to envelop you in a cool blanket as you look out towards an open tumultuous sea with waves that crash against ancient rock.

I could tell you about how the path to get to the beach during the middle of the day is as dark as the night because the mossy tree cover blocks all but the faintest hint of sunlight. While I would hope that you could paint a picture in your mind, the picture you paint would depend on if you have had experience with it or not.

Choosing a different form of communication, I could give you a few pictures. The pictures would communicate the scenery well because you would be able to see it with your own eyes. After all, a picture is worth a thousand words. However it would not be complete because I couldn't tell you why I felt the way I did. I could put it into words and describe it the way I perceived it. But it still couldn't communicate everything.

Now, I could set the pictures to a slide show with the text written underneath each slide. I am now communicating with more than one form of communication. You can now see each picture with the description I gave earlier. I have just increased the richness of the communication.

If I felt that, it still wasn't communicating well, I could set the slideshow to music. I can evoke the emotion associated with the music along with my picture slideshow. Furthermore, I could combine my audio visual slide show with me speaking the text. You could now hear the inflection of my voice and understand what I meant through the inflection you could hear in my voice. Finally, since I really want to communicate how I feel about the Oregon coast, I could record a video with me acting as your guide, along with the soundtrack and script that I have used earlier in the process. From the video, you can see how I carry myself and to how well I can communicate emotion through my eyes and body language.

Throughout the process I just described, I continued to add meaning to my message that I wanted to convey to you.   The meaning that I was able to add is referred to as richness. As I added more meaning to my message, I made my message richer. Fortunately, the Internet gives you the ability to add richness to your message unlike alternate forms of a communication medium such as paper. You can experiment with the various types of communication and see what works best for your online image.

With the Internet as a communication medium, you aren't limited to a cover letter or resume for job hunting.   You can present projects that you worked on with charts and graphs. You can show in detail how you saved your company a million dollars a year. It gives you the flexibility to show that you are special to your profession, while at the same time extending the amount of time that a HR person spends evaluating you as a job candidate. Without an online image, once the HR person is done with your resume, that may be all the face time you get.

If you are trying to impress Mrs. Right, maybe you can post a video with you doing what you do best. Video is a richer content medium than text because it communicates on many more levels. You can see all of the nonverbal communication, which makes up the majority of our communication. Unlike text, you could hear your voice and give an opportunity to solidify the all too critical first impression.

But with your online image, you don't always need to create ul-tra-rich content. A downside to using ultra-rich content is download time along with the time it takes to review your content goes up and people are unwilling to take the time to do so. But you can enhance your content using more than one form of communication.

Adding pictures to text, or a video here and there, can help your online image. One caveat, many people do not like music or video that starts immediately when they visit a web page. If you want to add that type of content, let people choose if they want to view your video or listen to a recording of you by making it available from a link.

CREATING CONTENT FOR THE RECOMMEND TOPICS

These categories and topics are intended to give you an idea of what should go. If you feel like you need to break out of the recom-mended categories, feel free. There is nothing that states an online image has to be this way or the highway. The reason those categories and topics are recommended is to provoke thought. To give you an idea what people *could* find when they come looking for your online image.

While these topics are named in an informal fashion consider renaming the topic from "my" to your name. For example, let's say your name is Jim. You would call the "my story" topic, "Jim's story." Changing the topic name can make it less personal and more formal, however referring to yourself as your formal name will help with search engine rankings. Search engines don't seem to find your profile if you always refer to yourself as Me, My, and I. You are simply choos-ing to refer to yourself in the third person rather than first person perspective. If you choose to refer to yourself in the third person perspective, you need to keep it consistent throughout most of your online image, with the exception of your blog.

THE MY STORY TOPIC

We all like hearing stories. It is how we tend to relate with one another. This topic is a chance to show very positive aspects of your life to date. If you can show growth from adversity, this is a great place to show what you encountered and how you grew from it. It all depends on how you want to present yourself. Your stereotype should be well communicated in your story. Refer to the structure diagram and remember to work in the characteristics you thought you could at the time you created the structure.

THE MY GOAL(S) TOPIC

Here is your chance to directly communicate what you are trying to accomplish in this life. This section is aimed squarely at your target audience. There is no room for ambiguity here. Be up-front with your goal(s) and tell the story as to why you want to accomplish that goal(s).

Make certain that you do not appear pushy with your goal. For instance, your end goal may be to get married and raise 2.3 children, but you could say that you are looking for a committed relationship. Still direct, but not Single White Female direct.

THE MY INTERESTS TOPIC

Working in characteristics that support your stereotype is a great use of the "my interests" topic. You can show some diversity in your interests here, after all you are human. Make sure that your interests don't communicate more than you want them to. For instance, if you say you are a member of the NRA, you are introducing an altogether new stereotype that may conflict with the stereotype you are trying to communicate.

PEOPLE DON'T READ WEB PAGES -SCANNING VERSES READING

On the Internet, people will often scan through the webpage they are visiting to get to the relevant information they searched for quickly. Typically people are looking for what they can click on to help them find what they are really looking for. Everything else on the web page to them is useless information. Unless, someone is really interested in the message you have put out on your website, they are not going to read all of your written content for comprehension.

But with an online image, most people are probably going to do a bit more reading than they do when they scan because they want to find out about you. However, you can make the reading easier for them by creating scannable text. Depending on the motive of the website visitor, some visitors will be searching for information that could help qualify you for a job while others are hell bent on finding reasons not to hire you. For an online image, we will make the assumption that the visitor is going to read everything so you are careful with every word that you type. Yet, at the same time you are going to make the page scannable by human eyes.

Creating scannable text is easy. To create scannable text you will need to focus on brevity in your text, identifying keywords and phrases, and providing clues as to the flow and meaning of the content.

Scannable text has the following characteristics

BOLD HEADINGS AND SUB HEADINGS

Creating bold headings and sub headings for placement throughout the text serves as a roadmap for the reader. This roadmap allows the reader to scan the webpage for the information they were looking for.

SHORT PARAGRAPHS

Long paragraphs make comprehension more difficult than concise and to-the point paragraphs. When you write text for a website, keep in mind that the reader is always scanning and not interested in reading a novel.   In this case, less truly is more.

SPACING BETWEEN PARAGRAPHS AND HEADINGS

Never underestimate the value of whitespace on a website. Adding an extra line of space after each paragraph and subheading will help break apart the monotony of a long narrative.

BOLD IMPORTANT KEY WORDS AND PHRASES

Identifying for the reader what you feel are the important ideas of the text. The reader should be able to read the bold words and get a quick feel what the content is about. Try to limit your bolding to a few selected words and/or key phrases per paragraph. The more you bold the harder it is to read because the bold words don't stand out as much as they once did.

USE LISTS TO MAKE IT EASIER TO READ IF YOU ARE LISTING MULTIPLE IDEAS IN A TOPIC.

Lists are clear and easier to read in list format than they are inside a paragraph. A reader's eye will be drawn naturally to a list as they read an article.

BILLY BOB'S STORY - WITHOUT SCANNABLE TEXT

Billy Bob Smith is a native of the city of Springfield, USA. Born and raised in Springfield, Billy Bob is currently attending Springfield high school where he maintains a 4.0 GPA. At his high school, Billy Bob is the student body president. Billy bob is quite active in the following activities: JROTC, Choir, Debate Team, Track and Field, and Wrestling. In choir, Billy bob was a featured soloist for the Choir on several occasions.

In 1998, Billy Bob's family was in a head on collision with a drunk driver. Everyone in Billy Bob's family survived thanks to Dr. Jane Doe. Dr. Doe witnessed the accident and rushed to the aide of the family. That moment will be forever etched in Billy Bob's life. Dr. Jane Doe is Billy Bob's inspiration for wanting to become a Doctor. Being able to help other people in their moment of need, like Dr. Doe did for Billy Bob's family, is why Billy Bob wants to be a medical doctor.

Billy Bob has dedicated his life to helping other people. In addition to Billy Bob's many extracurricular activities, Billy Bob is active as a volunteer in his local community as well as his church. As a big brother for the past four years, Billy Bob has been instrumental in helping two boys avoid a life of crime on the streets.

You were probably able to read that example and get the gist of the message. For illustration purposes, let's use the same text from above and turn it into a scannable version of Billy Bob Smith's Story.

WHO IS BILLY BOB SMITH - WITH SCANNABLE TEXT

*Billy Bob Smith is a **native** of the city of **Springfield, USA**. Born and raised in Springfield, Billy Bob is currently attending Springfield high school where he maintains a **4.0 GPA**.*

*At his high school, Billy Bob is the **student body president**.*

Billy bob is quite active in the following activities:

- *JROTC*
- *Choir*
- *Debate Team*
- *Track and Field*
- *Wrestling*

*In choir, Billy bob was a **featured soloist** on several occasions.*

Inspiration for Billy Bob's life

*In 1998, Billy Bob's family was in a **head on collision** with a drunk driver. Everyone in **Billy Bob's family survived thanks to Dr. Jane Doe**. Dr. Doe witnessed the accident and rushed to the aide of the family saving the life of Billy Bob's father.*

That moment will be forever etched in Billy Bob's memory. **Dr. Jane Doe is Billy Bob's inspiration** *for wanting to become a Doctor.*

Being able to help other people in their moment of need, like Dr. Jane Doe did for Billy Bob's family, is why **Billy Bob wants to be a medical doctor.**

Volunteering to help those in need

Billy Bob has **dedicated** *his life to* **helping other people.**

In addition to Billy Bob's many extracurricular activities, Billy Bob is active as a **volunteer** *in his local community as well as his church.*

As a big brother for the past four years, Billy Bob has been instrumental in **helping two boys** *avoid a life of crime on the streets.*

As you can see, scannable text helps people comprehend better by signaling what is important in the text to the reader. The subheadings help the reader by providing direction for the flow of the narrative. The eye is naturally drawn to the bolded words. By simply reading the bolded words, a reader can get the gist of an article very quickly.

BUILDING CONTENT FOR PEOPLE, NOT SEARCH ENGINES

Written content is the most important content type when it comes to helping search engines find your website. Search engines need to be able to analyze the content of the website in order to be able to classify the type of content on the page. When a search engine comes across text it can easily index the words it finds on the page and determine the importance of the page based on the text.

Search engines have their limitations when it comes to content. For the time being, search engines lack the ability to classify what is in an image, video, or sound. If they do classify images, the classification is based on the name of the image file and maybe the surrounding text, not the contents contained within the image.

Even more difficult for a search engine to classify is video or sound. To be able to determine content of video, search engines depend on meta data. Meta data is user supplied keywords which describe what would be appropriate for someone to search for to find the video.

A search engine's goal is to understand and categorize the text so that it returns accurate results. Someone who is trying to trick a search engine into returning a result will ultimately fail as search engines become aware of tactics used by people. Over time, search engines will get better at classifying text written for consumption by humans. For this reason alone, you should focus on creating good content.

Trying to improve your content so that someone can find you using the terms of your stereotype is not what you are trying to do. The only term you really want people to use to find you is your name. After all, you should be able to get the people who are checking your online image out to find you using your name or the web URL you have already given them. Your page is already relevant for your name. Your domain name with your full name in it, content on your website and page titles will help improve your rankings.

RULES FOR WRITING CONTENT FOR AN ONLINE IMAGE

Although it is improbable to anticipate all of the possible things you could write about on the web, there are some general rules to observe when creating any type of content .

RULE #1 - CONSIDER THE IMPACT TO YOUR ONLINE IMAGE

This is the overriding rule when it comes to your online image. You should never put out content that hurts or doesn't help you. All too often, people hastily put content out on the Internet before they have had a chance to consider its impact.   You should be asking yourself, does this support my online image or does it hurt my image.   If the content you would put out on the Internet makes you uneasy in any way, don't put it out there.   You should always look at content you create as an opportunity to enhance or build your online image.

RULE #2 - RESPECT THE LINE BETWEEN YOUR PUBLIC AND PRIVATE INFORMATION

During the conception phase, you spent a bit of time identifying the line between your public and personal life. Remind yourself before you create content, if this is something that you would be comfortable putting on a post card and mailing it across the country. If you are comfortable with the content, then feel free to post away.   However, if you are not comfortable with it, refine it to the point that you eliminate the elements which make you uncomfortable.

RULE #3 - RESPECT THE PRIVACY OF OTHERS

Here is your chance to use the Golden Rule — do unto others as you would have them do unto you. From a personal perspective, guard the privacy of those around you when it comes to writing about someone. Always ask permission to use someone's likeness in your online image.

Like people, companies want privacy too. Companies have a lot to lose when it comes to their online image. Companies invest millions of dollars in maintaining an image of their brand name. If you slander a company, you should expect effort made on their behalf to correct their image.   Companies typically respond with lawsuits, so be careful.

When it comes to your current or previous employers, don't reveal trade secrets or corporate secrets. Nothing can get you in hot water more than revealing trade secrets, but revealing corporate secrets comes close. Trade secrets are what companies use to create advantages for themselves. Corporate secrets include, but are not limited to, hiring and firing practices, policies, salary administration, benefit packages, and disciplinary actions.

RULE #4 - BE POSITIVE, DON'T GO NEGATIVE

While all of us go through phases in our lives where we want to complain about everything, the Internet is hardly the place for ranting. Even though some people may enjoy your complaints, find other outlets than the Internet. When we are feeling anger we can lose control when it comes to maintaining an online image. Negativity is a cancer which no one wants to introduce into any environment. Your spouse, employers you work for, and your children ultimately do not like to see you complain. Ninety-nine times out of a 100, people would much rather see you positive and upbeat about life rather than being negative about life.

The ability to respond positively to situations which would otherwise discourage a normal person is one of those universal characteristics of a quality individual.   By staying positive, you can avoid the pitfalls of being negative about a person, place or thing. Besides that, there are few things can hurt your career and online image more than singling out people for a public flogging. Although people might find your ranting entertaining, there is always a little voice in their back of their mind that tells them, "I'm next".

RULE #5 - LESS IS MORE.

The concept here is embodied by the colloquialism — if you give someone enough rope, they'll hang themselves. Likewise, if you take the opportunity to write content about everything under the sun, you may end up writing about something that will hurt your online image. Overwhelming a website visitor with everything you can possibly think of to tell them may overdo it in the visitors mind. Furthermore, by keeping a handle on the amount of content you have on your website, you can improve your message to make it clear and concise.

RULE #6 - AVOID HUMOR

Avoiding humor is one way to keep yourself from offending entire groups of people. Do not post any humor which could be considered bigoted, lewd, rude, crude, vulgar, sexist, and/ or racist. Those will be immediate warning signs to anyone evaluating you. Although in our day to day lives, humor is often welcome by most. Humor can be a double edged sword. Humor depends on the audience, culture, and context in order to be understood.

On the Internet you do not know who is viewing your online

image. With the danger of humor miscommunication being high, it best to leave it off an online image altogether. The one exception would be that if your goal is to become a comedian, then humor is your business and belongs all over your online image.

RULE #7 - BE A PERSON, NOT A PRODUCT

Sure, it helps to get you started in building your website, if you do think of yourself as a product. But, be interesting! You are a person and your online image should reflect that. An online image that treats you more like a product by using exaggerated claims or difficult or unintelligible language can give the visitor to your online image the wrong impression of you. All of us are fairly accustomed to being able to tell when we are hearing a sales pitch. Using language that presents you in a realistic light helps the targeted audience member relate to you as a person.

RULE #8 - IDENTIFY YOURSELF SO THEY KNOW WHO YOU ARE

This is the part where you don't want to play games. You need people to know who they are dealing with. Often your full name along with your city and state that you live in will be enough to identify who you are. However, if you have a common name, you may have a namesake in the same vicinity as you. You are going to need to further identify yourself. You will need to identify what is different between you and your local namesake and make certain that those aspects are trumped up.

RULE #9 - DON'T SHOW BIGOTRY

Hatred, Bigotry, racism, intolerance, and sexism, are some of the ugliest concepts in our modern culture. This is why so much effort in the past century has laid the framework to root these evils out of our society. If you want to be part of the 21st century, showing any characteristic like these will ruin any chance you have for employment with a company. You will become a liability and companies tend to avoid people like that. Unless, of course, it becomes in vogue to be bigoted against other people. For some reason, I don't see that happening.

RULE #10 - DON'T POST ANYTHING ABOUT ILLEGAL BEHAVIOR

While this rule may go without saying, there are enough examples of people out on the Internet who have lost their jobs, their marriages, and freedom as a result of posting illegal activity. Illegal behavior can be underage drinking and smoking, vandalism, theft like downloading pirated music, movies, and/or software along any other sort of crime. Don't incriminate yourself by posting this garbage on the Internet. If you participate in illegal behavior, stop. And if for some reason you can't, get help from the proper authorities. If you are foolish enough to do it, then you will reap what you sow.

RULE #11 - AVOID THE APPEARANCE OF EVIL

On the Internet, you need to be clear about who you are. If you have paraphernalia of activities that could be misinterpreted by people as behavior which would give your online image negative characteristics, you should not post it. Paraphernalia comes in many forms. For example, if you are a married man and you blog about how much you like a particular dating site, you will make you online image look like an adulterer. Another example could be a teenager writing about her favorite file sharing software. Although there are legitimate reasons (not many) for file sharing networks, most people equate file sharing to stealing pirated music. Keep the paraphernalia of activities that could hurt your online image away from the Internet.

RULE #12 - DON'T WRITE WHEN YOU ARE ANGRY OR OTHERWISE IMPAIRED

When passions run high, common sense can go out the window. For Online Image Management, you need to be thinking about how this makes you look and not how badly you could make someone else look. In moments of anger, you may be likely to dump whatever you are feeling at the time on to the Internet. If you do need to vent, keep it in your private life, far away from the Internet.

BLOGGING

While much has been said about the dangers of publishing on the Internet, blogging or posting frequent updates to your website is a great tool for your online image. Blogging has many positive aspects which enhance your online image if done correctly. Often, blogging can be a fantastic way to show your grasp of a subject matter. By blogging/writing accurately on the subject matter, this will enhance your credibility as a knowledgeable resource on the topic. Showing yourself as a knowledgeable resource for a topic which encompasses characteristics of your stereotype, strengthens your stereotype.

Blogging gives you the ability to showcase your ability to communicate through writing. Writing on the Internet on a frequent basis can show that you can communicate with people in written form. Furthermore, if you have a writing style which is interesting to read, you may be able to draw regular subscribers to your blog.

Showing that you have a good writing style is a desirable characteristic of any human being which will work well in your stereotype. If you do not consider yourself to have a good writing style or you think you are lucky to string together a sentence, don't worry. Many people will help you with writing and several resources are available on the Internet to help with writing. At a minimum, you can comment on what other people have written about topics which would enhance your stereotype.

Yet there is an ugly side to blogging. The typical nature of bloggers is to mind dump into their blog. I call this approach, the "box of chocolates" approach to blogging. You know, the often quoted line from the movie Forest Gump, "My Momma always said, life is like a box of chocolates. You never know what your gunna get." This approach is dangerous to an online image because, like the line in the movie, you never know what you are going to get. If left to the whims of your mood, you might end up blogging about what you did last night, and then later blog about your terrible boss. You can see mind dumping in action. It's as easy as going out to the Internet and searching for some blogs. You should try it. Everybody else is doing it. And it's super fun.

It is true that blogging tends to get a considerable amount of bad press. Blogging only receives bad press because of all the bonehead things that people are doing or saying on their blogs. Blogging certainly does not receive the bad press because it's a bad technology. (The blogging concept is great in the sense that it democratizes the distribution of information away from the major media outlets.) Fortunately, you already know to protect yourself by creating content that only reflects who you want to be on the Internet.

However, you will always need to guard against the urge to write about whatever is on your mind. Be calculating in your approach to your blog. Thus, only write about topics which reinforce your online image. Writing on personal items is probably not in your best interest on your online image blog. When you blog be sure to research the topic you are writing about. Although you might not be an expert of the industry, blogging will build your credibility while at the same time helping you learn more about the topics that you are blogging about. Who knows, one day you could become the expert everyone is quoting on their blogs.

HANDING OVER THE CONTENT TO YOUR DESIGNER

Before you hand over your content to your designer, review your content as you would if you were reviewing a resume. Check for misspellings, grammatical errors, and typos. Give the content the review it needs and illicit peer review as well. A fresh set of eyes can't hurt you when it comes to reviewing content. Often they will catch things that you missed after several reviews.

Your designer will have their own process for getting your content to them. Talk to your designer about the format they want your content in. For example, do they need it in Word or Excel? Once they get your content in the format they would like, this should be all that your designer needs to put it into your website. However, if you want to create advanced content like video or audio you will need to communicate with your designer as to what you want. Your designer should be able to tell you if what you want to do is within the realm of possibility. Additionally, if you are going to create multimedia content by yourself, your designer will need to tell you which file format they need your multimedia content in. I would recommend you let your designer build your multimedia content if you choose to have it. They will be more likely to keep it within the theme of your website.

❧ STEP 6 — EVALUATING THE FINISHED PRODUCT ❧

You have made it to the point where your web designer has told you that your site is finally ready to go and wants you to review it. This will be your first opportunity to take a look at your online image. Overall, you should be happy with the finished product. You paid good money to have your online image designed. If necessary, ask for revisions, but remember this time around it is minor revision. For instance, a minor revision is asking for a menu items text to be changed, while a major revision is stating that you don't like the overall layout of the website and want it redone. At this point in the process, your designer and you will have gone through quite a bit of work. Your designer is likely to balk at the prospect of having to do a major revision to the design. Especially when you consider, that you had the opportunity to review it before the designer went to all the work to build the website.

When you review your site, pay attention to what message the website conveys. Think of your online image as a resume. Much effort is spent proofreading your resume because of the importance people place on accuracy within your resume. If you hand a resume littered with misspellings to an employer, it communicates that you do not know how to produce quality work. Inattention to detail on a resume is practically an unforgivable sin in the corporate world. Because you didn't take the steps to present yourself as best as you can, your resume wouldn't get more than a 10 second look.

With an online image, if you don't pay attention to the detail of your website you could be setting yourself up for failure. The online image you present to the world would be like going to an interview dressed to the hilt with food stains all over your clothing. Your stains on your clothing would speak louder than your credentials. Stains on your online image will have the same effect. Certainly, you wouldn't have gone to the expense to hire a designer, write all the content, and then not give your online image the scrutiny it needs to be highly reflective of your capabilities. Your online image needs to communicate your stereotype, not a stereotype of someone who can't produce quality work.

LOOK FOR CLARITY

You need to see if the designer has captured your stereotype in the design. When you look at the design, do you see something that communicates what your overall stereotype is supposed to be? Or rather, do you see something that is counter to what an online image should be? For instance, if you are an accountant and want to be a CFO one day, do you see a CFO when you look at the online image or do you see hair stylist?

Another way to see if the website provides the clarity is by looking at whether or not the website clearly identifies you as the subject. Remembering the goal is for your target audience to feel like they have found your website. Based on minimal information the target audience member needs to make a clear determination, that yes, this is the person I am checking up on.

CONSISTENCY

Every web page within the website should be recognizable as your online image. One of the key checks you need to perform is checking for consistency from page to page. A good website should have a standard theme and carry that theme throughout the entire site. Often, this is expressed as a standard design for every page. All pages share the same menu structure as well as the same color scheme for the website. The only exception to consistency throughout the website, is sometimes designers will design a splash screen for the home page of your website. If a designer chooses to use a splash screen, the look should be fairly close to the rest of the pages. The splash screen may lack a menu structure, but is should have the same color scheme and contain design elements from the main design.

CHECK WEBSITE FOR BROKEN LINKS, MISSPELLINGS, TYPOS, GRAMMAR, AND OTHER MINUTIA.

Although you should have checked your content for grammatical errors, misspellings, and typos before you sent it to the designer, it is always a good idea to re-review for those types of errors.

Further, review every page for broken links. A broken link is when the link that you click on does not take you to the appropriate webpage or takes you to one that doesn't exist. Just because you checked the links on one page does not mean that all the links work on every page. Every page should be treated as its own set of links. Web pages typically are created from a template, but for your assurance that you have no broken links, you will want to check this out. Click on every link to make sure that they go to the appropriate location. There are automated tools which can do the link verification for you. You can find those tools by searching for "link verification software".

MAKING SURE YOU GOT EVERYTHING YOU WANTED

You know your content best, after all you created it. Sometimes, when the designer copies and pastes your content from a word processor, the designer may miss some piece of text or lose formatting. If something is missing make a note and tell the designer after you have finished reviewing. Furthermore, once you see your content laid out on screen, does it look like what you envisioned? Does it communicate as well as you wanted or is it distracting? Asking these questions now will help you take the view that you are ultimately responsible for the appearance of your online image.

PEER REVIEW

You should always engage the opinion of two or three people who will give you valuable feedback. Ideally, these people will be in your target audience. After all, the target audience has the greatest likelihood of seeing the stereotype you are trying to present. This feedback you gain from your reviewer can shape the direction of your online image. Have them review your online image for inaccuracies and stereotype fit. Ask them to record their opinions on the entire website. They should write down their initial impressions using adjectives to describe the person they are viewing, what type of person you are, and what they think your goals are for your online image.

As the reviewers go through every page on the site, have them record the characteristics of the stereotype as they are communicated on the page. Further, ask them to record any difficulties they had with your website such as difficulty finding information, broken links, and confusing information. Once your peers finish, compare what they wrote down to what you said you wanted to accomplish with each page. You'll want to know if you hit the mark or if you've got work to do. Obviously, people are going to use different adjectives than you did to try to describe what they saw. The comparison needs to be made to see if they came close. For instance, if you are trying to convey "I am a high school student who wants to be a doctor" and your reviewer came up with "High school student who want to be in medical field" then you win. You did it. You got the reviewer to see what you wanted them to see.

TRAINING ON HOW TO USE YOUR WEBSITE, BLOG, EDITING TOOLS, AND SITE STATISTICS.

Before you have the keys handed over to your new web site, make certain you understand how to use your new website. Nothing is worse than taking ownership of a website and then feeling intimidated at the prospect of maintaining the website.

You should be trained to do the following duties:

- ✓ How to log into your website.
- ✓ How to manage your blog.
- ✓ How to restrict access to any particular content.
- ✓ How to add a new page to the website.
- ✓ How to add a new category (if possible).
- ✓ How to link from one page to another.
- ✓ How to upload content, like an image to your website.
- ✓ How to categorize a blog posting.
- ✓ How to edit a previously created blog posting.
- ✓ How to back up your website.

Don't let the designer off the hook. Have them help you until you have a thorough understanding of what you need to do. Most importantly, take detailed notes. After the designer leaves you on that day, you may never get another opportunity to ask questions again and you'll be left on your own to figure it out.

SUMMING IT ALL UP

In this step you created your online image. Throughout the build phase you should have incorporated all of the elements of your online image. You should be proud of yourself, you took control of your digital representation. You know are ready to announce yourself to the world in the next phase of Online Image Management.

CHAPTER NINE

PROMOTION PHASE OF ONLINE IMAGE MANAGEMENT

"Next to doing the right thing, the most important thing is to let people know you are doing the right thing."

—*John D. Rockefeller, American Industrialist*

When it comes to information placed on the Internet, it's as if we all live in a small town called Netville. In Netville, if someone in town knows something about what you did the other night, soon everyone in town will know. The more risqué the action, the more quickly the gossip spreads. Unfortunately, truth has little to do with whether or not the gossip is spread. As Winston Churchill once said, "A lie gets halfway around the world before the truth has a chance to get its pants on." So in this small town of Netville, you must be very careful about what you do in public and who you tell about your actions. You must manage your reputation or run the risk of others managing your reputation for you. As a citizen of Netville, you need to help people see you in the most positive light possible, short of walking on water. (If you can walk on water that really helps your reputation, not to mention all the YouTube hits your video will get.)

This phase is about building credibility for your online image while at the same time announcing yourself to the world. By now, your website is up and running and serves as the best digital representation of you on the Internet. However, your website can only show up as one of the search results in most search engines. Being limited to one result is almost like your website being a needle in a haystack. To build a complete online image you need additional resources on the Internet which validate your stereotype as well as show up individually in the search results. To do so, you will need to get more than just your website to show up in the top results. You will need to spread your message throughout the Internet in places where it makes sense.

In essence, the efforts of this phase are intended to build the reputation for your online image. You will want your reputation to communicate your chosen stereotype and establish your credibility. By putting yourself out on the Internet in carefully selected locations, you will help people see you as your stereotype as well as building credibility. The more places that support your online image the more likely it is people will see you as being a credible professional.

TWO PRINCIPLES

There are two principles which you will use to build your online image's reputation. The first principle of online image promotion is the stereotype principle. With an online image, your reputation on the Internet is what other people validate your online image with. People need to see you acting as your stereotype on the Internet. You need to be on the Internet posting content, which can be easily identified as yours, where people expect your stereotype to be.

The second principle of online image promotion is the "If everyone else is jumping off the cliff, I guess I should too," principle.

Let's refer to this principle as the lemming principle.   People, in general, will tend to believe something is credible if multiple people say the same things about it.   For instance, if you are trying to evaluate which car dealership to purchase your next vehicle from, you are likely to get input from multiple sources.   The first source would be the car dealerships wanting to sell you a shiny new car. ABCXYZ car dealership advertises that they are "the best car dealership around." For our purposes, let's say that they truly are the best car dealership around. However, the skeptic in you automatically dismisses the car dealership's advertising because they are *supposed* to tell you that they are the best car dealership around. At this point in the car buying process, ABCXYZ car dealership has little to no credibility in your mind to support their claim of being "the best car dealership around."

In order for you to believe ABCXYZ car dealership, you need to hear positive references from impartial sources. Now, let's suppose you ask a few of your friends about which car dealership they like. If everyone you ask seemingly backs up the car dealership's claim, you now see the car dealership as the best dealership for buying a car.   So why, when in the beginning of the process you were told by the car dealership that they were the best car dealership, didn't it matter? You still needed the opinions of other people to validate the car dealership's claim in your mind.   But why? Most people's opinions are very subjective and often ill informed. It's the fact that you heard it from someone who has had experience with the car dealership and has nothing to gain from giving the car dealership a positive reference.   The same concept is true for your online image. You need other sources validating your online image.

How can you find people who will be willing to help you out with building your reputation? Rather than pay people to be your friends, turn to your social network.   Your social network is the best place to get people to help build your online image's reputation.

OVERALL TECHNIQUE

As a general principal for promotion, the more you have out on the Internet about you, the easier it is to find you. Search engines have a higher likelihood of indexing your name if they can find it in more places. In other words, if your website exists and no search engine knows it exists, does it truly exist?

So you need the help of a search engine to get your online image out there. Only one problem exists. Seemingly, no one outside of the search engine companies really knows how search engines determine what pages are more relevant when it comes to returning results. Sure there are ideas on how to optimize the search engine results, but remember search engines are trying to mimic the human thought process on determining relevance.

Like humans, if a search engine sees more references to elements of your online image, they are going to determine that your online image is more relevant than other pages that have the same terms in them. Through prominent placement of key words that will be searched to find you (your name, location, website address, e-mail, etc.) search engines will be able to find the reference to your online image.

Placing multiple comments on the Internet will help fill the top 30 results with the results you want to be there. By taking advantage of the web 2.0 features of websites which allow commentary, you can spread your online image's reputation to enough locations so that the likelihood of inclusion in the top 30 results is much higher. Overall, you will want these multiple references for your online image to point back to the main source of your online image, your website. Everything you place out on the Internet needs to contain a link back to your website. You need to treat your website as the center of your online image universe.

What you are attempting to do is to help your target audience see your stereotype. You will want to put your comments in areas where it makes sense for your target audience to be looking for you. This means you are going to seek out the gathering places for similar people of your stereotype.   Additionally, you are going to depend on search engine results to draw your target audience to places they may not normally gather.

The promotion phase is broken into three steps which will cover the important areas for online image promotion.

- Step 1: Announcing yourself to the world
- Step 2: Applying the stereotype principle
- Step 3: Applying the lemming principle

Your Website: Center of your Online Image Universe

STEP 1 — ANNOUNCING YOURSELF TO THE WORLD

Getting your target audience to know you exist is an essential element to achieving the goals of your online image. People aren't likely to call you out of the blue and ask you for your website address. You need to get your website out there and make it clear to your target audience that you have a website ready to help them make the right decision about you.   To do so, you will need to incorporate your online image into your life and submit your website to the top three search engines.

INCORPORATE YOUR ONLINE IMAGE INTO YOUR LIFE

Your online image should be promoted when you reach out to your target audience.   To promote your online image, use your website address in any correspondence with your target audience.   Any correspondence would include documents like letters, e-mails, essays, resumes, business cards, cover letters, and college applications.   In the case of a resume, displaying your website address prominently next to your contact information is one way you can cleverly get the attention of a target audience member.

When you put references to your website on any correspondence, you can choose to make the reference so obvious the website address stands out. Or you can make the inclusion subtle using the same font the rest of your correspondence is formatted with.   Only you will be able to tell which style is appropriate for you and your target audience.   In general, if your target audience is conservative in nature, you should go with the subtle approach.   Conversely, if your target audience expects something flashy, then give them what they are looking for.

To illustrate this concept, look at this as if you are preparing materials for a job search.   At this point in the process, you already have a website which serves as the foundation for your online image. You should attempt to draw your target audience to your website where you have gone into additional depth to support your job search efforts.   When you prepare materials for a job search, adding your URL to your resume should be the first place you start. In addition to updating your skills and your job history, you need to update your contact information to include your website address.   Simply putting your website address in the proper format starting with the http://,(e.g. , http://www.not-a-domain.xyz) will communicate that you have a website with additional materials for the targeted audience member's consideration.

Next, you should use your cover letter as another correspondence which you can include references to your website. Writing up a brief sentence touting what's available on your website will pique their interest and draw them to your website. If you have chosen to use password protected areas of your website, make certain you communicate the password to your target audience in your cover letter. This sort of password-protected, forbidden zone that only the recipient of your cover letter is allowed to go into will draw out their natural curiosity. Giving your password out along with a description of the benefits of logging on to the website is best accomplished when it is included on the correspondence that has the website address.

Finally, if you are communicating with a perspective employer via e-mail, add your website address to your e-mail signature. Your e-mail signature is the piece of text that can be added to every e-mail you send. Creating a signature which includes your website address draws attention to your online image. It's just another way to drive home the point that you have a website and that you want people to go to it.

Keep in mind that with e-mail if you send your website address to your friends they will likely tie themselves to you by including the link to your website from their MySpace, Facebook or blog page. This may be fine, but keep in mind the goal of your online image. If it fits within the goal of your online image to have your friends as part of your online image, go ahead and send your website address to all of your friends. Otherwise, only purposefully include your website address on e-mails when your target audience is involved.

The approach outlined above for communicating with an employer, can be used with any target audience. With any target audience, you exchange some type of correspondence to alert them to your desires. For instance, if you are applying for college, you may submit an application. Further, if you are meeting a potential business partner for lunch, you may exchange business cards. The pattern is the same. When you give materials to a member of a target audience, make sure the material you give has your website address on the material.

In some cases it might be considered pushy or taboo to include your website address. For instance, if your online image is to help you get Mrs. Right you may not want to include your website address with your phone number. It might be seen as being too forward or pushy.   When you decide not to give out a website address, you are going to depend upon your online image being found with a name search for you.

SUBMITTING TO SEARCH ENGINES

You will want to ensure that your website appears somewhere in the top 30 search engine results. Submitting your website's address to the search engine, places your website into the search engine's queue of websites it needs to index. The website you just built is most likely a new website that no one, including search engines, really knows about. Since you don't want to leave it up to chance, you need to submit your website address to the major search engines for indexing.

The great part about search engine submission and ranking is it is free. You shouldn't have to pay for submission or ranking of your website to search engines. If a search engine allows website addresses to be submitted, they offer this as a free service to everyone.   Further, no one can promise the number one search ranking for any of the top three search engines. Only the search engine companies manage the results, and the top 3 search engine companies do not sell rankings. Anyone who tells you that you they can guarantee a top ranking is trying to make a quick buck off you.

The best way to find out how to submit a website address to the search engine is to search for the phrase, "submit a website address". At the time of writing this book the website URLs for the top three search engines are:

- **Google** - http://www.google.com/addurl/
- **Yahoo** - https://siteexplorer.search.yahoo.com/submit
- **Bing** - http://www.bing.com/docs/submit.aspx

It will take time for your website to start showing up in search engines. Depending on the search engine, it can be as quick as a few days or it can take up to a month. A good way to test whether or not your website has been indexed by a search engine is to search for your website address. If you get your website back in the search results, you will know the search engine has seen your website. If you haven't seen your website show up for some time, you can always resubmit the website to the search engine for indexing.

ADVERTISING ON SEARCH ENGINES

Another great way to get noticed on search engines is to pay for advertising. The positive aspect of this approach is it gets your website on the first page with little effort. Advertising works well when you have a very common name (Joe Smith) or share your name with a celebrity or public figure. Furthermore, advertising can be an effective way to strengthen your stereotype, since advertising shows confidence in who you are and the mindset that only important people would bother advertising.

To illustrate the benefits of advertising, consider what advertising could do for someone who has a very common name. For example, let's use someone named Joe Smith. (A quick Google exact search using "Joe Smith" *in quotes* returns over 1.5 million hits. By comparison, an uncommon name using quotes yields less than 10 hits.) Anyone named Joe Smith is competing against celebrities, professional athletes, a former congressman, and the Mormon prophet, as well as anyone else named Joe Smith. With that much competition, the task of showing up in the top 30, let alone the top 10 search results is daunting.

But wait, there is hope. Joe can turn to advertising to promote his online image. Notice that on the search for "Joe Smith", no one is advertising. This presents an awesome opportunity for Joe. He can use advertising to promote his name on the cheap. By targeting the search term "Joe Smith", Joe can place advertisements which will guarantee first page billing. Since Joe doesn't want to pay for advertising all of the time, Joe activates his advertising campaign when he is looking for consulting work or new employment. Now, Joe appears when he wants to and how he wants to. He is no longer at the mercy of search engines to determine how relevant his website is. Automatically, Joe has improved his online image by getting his stereotype (Professional Human Resources Manager) and his target audience (Fortune 500 companies) on the first result page which returns his name.

Always remember your stereotype before you consider any type of advertising. While it is quick and easy to get to the top, it has a few downsides. Advertising may not be appropriate for your stereotype and it is not free. Keep in mind, for many stereotypes you want to be seen as a person and not a product. For instance, if you are a marketing or sales representative, you might see it as advantageous to have your online image show up in the top spot of the advertisements. Having your name show up near the top of the advertisement space shows you can do what it takes to get people to notice you. On the other hand, some jobs such as a police officer, may not want to be seen advertising their online image. Use your best judgment, you'll know what to do.

Similar to advertising with a newspaper, you create an advertisement with a headline and one or two sentences. Then you specify with the search engine company which keywords that you want the advertisement returned with. It can be as simple as using your name as the keywords you want to target, for example "Aaron Francesconi" would be the keywords I would use in an advertising campaign. The company may suggest a price that you need to pay to for your ad show up in the rankings. The nice part about how the ads work, is you only pay the bid price if someone clicks on your link. Search engines generally, do not charge you if no one clicks on your link. Keep in mind, if you choose highly desirable keywords which many people want to use, you will have to pay more. The search engine companies use a system where the highest bidder for the keyword wins the most prominent placement. However, you can still show up on the first page and not be the top bidder. All you need to do is be on the first page. The search engine company will have tools you need to help place your advertisement where you want it to be and contain costs.

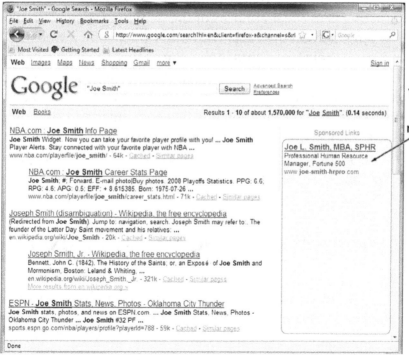

You can appear on the first result page and automatically improve your Online Image

To start advertising, go to the search engine you want to advertise with and search for the name of the search engine and the word, advertising. For example, use the term "Google Advertising" on Google. Look for the result belonging to the search engine company somewhere in the top 5 results. The search engine companies will provide you with detailed instruction about how advertising works with them.

STEP 2: APPLYING THE STEREOTYPE PRINCIPLE

When you interact with people, usually the only trace of that interaction is in the memories of the people involved. On the Internet when a person interacts with other people on a website, they often leave their footprints in the places that they have been which can be found for years to come. When building your online image's reputation you will want to leave your footprints with a calculated approach. Strategically, you will be choosing your targets carefully, posting things which can be tied back to you easily on other websites, and only posting things which are appropriate for your stereotype to be posting.

WHERE TO PLACE REFERENCES TO YOUR ONLINE IMAGE.

There are multiple places that you can put references to your online image. From companies that want you to comment on their sites, to social networking websites, there are a myriad of locations where you can put references to your online image. The nice part about all of this, is you do not have to create other websites. You can utilize the capabilities of other people's websites. Many websites are trying to solicit your commentary because they know it adds value to their website.   Likewise, adding your commentary to their website adds value to your online image.   It is a win-win relationship between you and the websites with web 2.0 features.

Recognizing web 2.0 features on regular websites is easy once you know what to look for. Website owners want you to comment on products, articles, blog posts, and anything else their site features. As such, the website owner typically places the web 2.0 features on whatever they value most.   For instance, if you are on a retailer website like walmart.com you will find the postings on an individual product. Furthermore, a news organization website like cnn.com, allows you to write comments on articles.

Web 2.0: What to Look for

POSTREPLY ⬈

4 Comments Add a Comment

Add your comment

POST A COMMENT   Create your own review

Rate and review this product

Discuss Story

Guest Reviews

Write an online review and share your thoughts with other guests. See all Reviews

Recent comments

There are two components to web 2.0 commenting technologies. First, there is a place to add your comments and second, you can read what other people have commented. That's it. To find where you can comment on a particular website, you are looking for places on the web page which allow user comments, discussion, or otherwise solicit your involvement. Typically, you can find areas to comment towards the bottom or end of a webpage.   Look for tell-tale phrases such as, "Write Review", "Be the first to review this product", "Create your own review", "Add your comment", "Join the discussion", "Customer Ratings and Reviews". Once you find the place to comment, all you have to do is write your highly applicable comment.

The second component to a web 2.0 commenting technology is the ability to read comments. Once a person leaves feedback, you should be able to read their comments that have been added on that page. In order for the strategies of this phase to work, search engines need to be able to find and index comments. If comments are not displayed, then you are not able to take advantage of the commenting feature on the website.

When you find a website you think you should leave a trace of your online image on, consider the impact of where you are placing content and what it does for your online image. Look at the type of website you are going to associate yourself with. The reputation of the website can reflect badly upon you if it doesn't make sense for your stereotype to be there. You wouldn't want to tie your reputation to a website that is thought of as a website for children on the web unless of course, your stereotype should be there. For instance, John Jacob Jingleheimer-Schmitt is trying to present himself as a leading executive. If John adds comments to websites that pertain to how to "stick it to the man", John ends up doing his online image a disservice. First, an executive would rarely want to "stick it to the man" because they, in fact, are the "man". Second, it doesn't fit the mold of an executive stereotype to fight against the corporate establishment, rather an executive stereotype would work within the establishment to improve it. Thus, if John were to provide ample ways of how to theoretically "stick it to the man", then he would do severe damage to his online image, as well as his goal of attaining executive leadership. John would be well advised to leave his online image off those types of websites.

Additionally, you will need to evaluate the nature of the comments on the website. Just because you found a website which would support your stereotype it doesn't mean you should tie yourself to the website. If for some reason the comments do not appear to be moderated by anyone, you run the risk of having someone come in and post garbage on the bulletin board. Think of it as yet another opportunity for spammers to put their junk mail all over the web. Garbage could run the gamut from selling prescription Viagra to sex sites. Unless your goal is to be seen as the largest seller of prescription drugs over the Internet, this sort o' garbage around your profile does nothing for you.

As a way to illustrate this point, let's use a fictional person named Mary Trendsetter, who is focusing on becoming the leading fashion designer in New York City, wants to improve her online image. Mary is extremely knowledgeable in fashion design and she wants to use this to her advantage. Following the guidelines, she starts commenting on fashion websites. Eventually she comes across a website which has some great articles on fashion design and web 2.0 features.

Example: Unmoderated comments

Thoughts anyone?

Re: Contacting the site owner
by john-jacob-jingleheimer-schmitt on Thu Oct 09, 2008 8:40 pm

Online image management is the best thing since sliced bread. This book has helped me in so many ways. I really like the part about adding comments. Thank you Mr. Francesconi! Check my online image out http://www.johnjacobjingleheimer-schmitt.com. Now people can see who the real John Jacob Jingleheimer-Schmitt is.
John Jacob Jingleheimer-Schmitt
Springfield, USA

An unmoderated forum can hurt your Online Image and help you find cheap Viagra

Re: Contacting the site owner
by online-rx on Thu Oct 16, 2008 6:32 pm

Sorry for interrupting you, but this information
is very important for your purse and family budget!
Don't pay a lot for medications, we offer acceptable prices.
For example, Viagra doesn't cost 160$ for 10 pill!
It's deception!
We offer you Viagra (10 pils x 100 mg) + Ciallis (10 pills x 20 mg) only 68.72$ - that's the real price.

You can see the whole list of medications on our site.

Display posts from previous: [All posts ▼] Sort by [Post time ▼] [Ascend]

POSTREPLY ↵

However upon further inspection, Mary notices every once in a while, the moderators of the site have allowed spam in the comment areas. In particular, Mary notices spam ads for weight loss, male enhancement, and prescription drugs. Spam ads indicate that Mary would be wise to avoid commenting on this site because it appears to allow anything and everything to be posted. Even if the ads may not contain damaging information today, the comments are not moderated. Mary's online image could be at risk because of what someone could later post.

HOW TO ADD COMMENTS

In writing comments, adhere to the outlined guidelines for writing content from the build phase. To support your stereotype, you need to make certain that what you comment on is directly applicable to your stereotype. There should be no question as to why you commented on the product or article. As you know, comments that are directly applicable to your stereotype, reinforces your stereotype thus lending additional credibility to your online image.

Write unique, insightful, well-written comments on whatever you happen to be commenting on. Unique comments show that you took the time to consider what you were going to say. Furthermore, unique comments will end up in the descriptive text beneath the search engine result items. Insightful comments show that you have a fresh perspective. You should evaluate how comments are added on the page. At a glance, you should be able to see what the system allows in term of identifying who you are. Looking at the user area for commenting you should be able to see if you can use your real name as the person who posted the information.

Furthermore, if you have the ability to include an e-mail address, you should. E-mail addresses are unique, so when someone searches for you with an e-mail address they will be able to find your comments easily. A word of caution, unscrupulous people create programs to search the Internet for e-mail addresses. After they collect e-mail addresses they start sending spam to those e-mail addresses. However, I believe the benefits of putting your e-mail address into comments outweigh the risk of getting more spam. After all, most mail programs have spam filtering. The best way to mitigate the risk is to use an e-mail address that is solely for the purposes of your on-line image.

Finding ways to work in your website address into comments will be very helpful to you in promoting your online image. If someone in your target audience were to stumble across your comment you have written, wouldn't it be great if they could quickly go find out more about you. Having your website address in the comment gives them the ability to quickly visit your website.

In the example comment below, notice how John was able to work in his name, location, e-mail, and website address. All of this information will help search engines index the comment so that it can be successfully attributed to John's online image.

An Example Comment

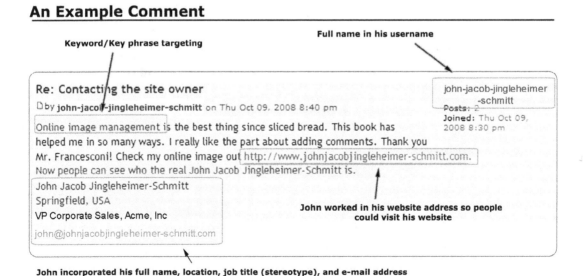

John incorporated his full name, location, job title (stereotype), and e-mail address

FINDING TRADE SPECIFIC SITES

Many industries have user groups or bulletin boards where you can write and discuss your trade with other like-minded professionals. Seek out trade websites that are specific to your stereotype.   For example, an engineer should seek out the places that engineers come together on the Internet.   Since engineers are specialized, they should drill down until they find their specific specialty. The more knowledgeable they seem about something the more credible their online image becomes. Seeing their footprint on these sites further reinforces their stereotype.

One caveat, if you participate in discussions on trade sites, make sure you do not put information which will lead you to possible confrontation with other members of your community. To illustrate this point, let's use someone named Timothy Beancounter. Tim is an accountant and a good one at that. Tim goes onto an accounting forum to discuss accounting things. While browsing through some very captivating threads on the benefits of using Activity Based Costing, Tim finds an Enron thread on the discussion board. Upon further review, some of the participants on the message board are actually defending the creative accounting that Enron was doing. While tempting to get into the fray, Tim should tread with caution. While Tim may be able to write a professional response that counters the bogus opinions, what would Tim do if they respond negatively? Does Tim escalate his comments or does he leave well enough alone? It certainly would be horrible for Tim's future or current employer to see that he can't keep the peace in a professional forum. The conclusion any employer could make may hurt Tim in his current job and future endeavors.

The best choice is to stay away from discussions which could bring out negative characteristics of an individual. Remember, that you are trying to bring out positive characteristics of a quality individual and your stereotype. Being caught up in the fray of a heated discussion would make it difficult to present those positive characteristics.

COMMENTING ON PRODUCTS YOU HAVE PURCHASED

Many retail websites offer web 2.0 features on their websites to boost sales.   Companies understand the value of people commenting on products.   In the end, their customers are happier because customers are helping customers avoid products which do not live up to expectations.   Commenting on products which you have experience with, helps improves credibility of your online image as well as improves the comments on the product.

There are multiple products that would support a stereotype. Products which would be the associated as the paraphernalia of your stereotype will be a good place to start with when trying to support your online image.   For instance, Timothy Beancounter, our accountant example, might have pretty strong opinions on which financial calculator is the best one to use. When you are seen associating with the tools of the trade, you automatically build your credibility.

Commenting on books which your stereotype should be interested, provides an excellent opportunity for you to build your online image.   Be sure to comment on books directed at a subject matter which your online image should be interested in.   Books provide a way to show that you stay current in your field and that you care enough about your field to take the time to stay up to date.

Consider what commenting on an accounting book could do for Timothy Beancounter's online image.   Timothy can selectively target books which happen to be in vogue within the accounting profession. If he were to pick up a book on the Enron scandal from an accounting point of view, Timothy could write about the strong points of the book. After Timothy finishes reading the book, he should write a well thought out review. If he were to post this review for the book on a site like Amazon.com, he will improve his online image.   Timothy needs to be cautious of his tone when he writes a book review as to not come across in a manner which would not be fitting of his accountant stereotype.

USING SOCIAL NETWORKING SITES

Social networking websites give you an opportunity to use sites which people use to find other people, and draw them back to your online image website.   You can use these sites to provide minimal information about yourself, but in the end, draw them back to your website.   While it is tempting to put additional information on these social networking websites, it's often better to stay away from doing so.   Your efforts to build a quality image was done with your website and attempting to make an additional resource for people to use to find out about you runs the risk of you losing sight of your goal.   Any social networking site you use should be only used to draw people back and to strengthen your online image.   If you attempt to add more to the social networking site such as personal content you run the risk of dilution of your online image.

When you use social networking websites, you may have friends contact you wanting to be listed as one of your friends.   It may be hard for you to tell them no without damaging your friendship.   Since much of the information on these social networking sites is potentially public, you need to guard against crossing the line between your public and private life.   The danger in social networking sites is when you allow yourself to let your guard down and show yourself as the "after hours" you with your friends.   Of course, this isn't a problem when your friends enhance your online image.   But for the majority of us, our friends are not going to help our professional online image.

In the protection phase, you will be introduced to the concept of using an alternate persona to take full advantage of social networking from a social standpoint. Keep it simple for now by copying some text from your website and posting your website address on these social networking sites to build your credibility.

As an example, let's use a fictional college student named Carol Undergrad. Carol uses her social networking sites on MySpace and Facebook only to draw people back to her website.   She provides some text which she copied from her website, along with a professional photograph, and a highly prominent link to her website.   Carol does not use her name to socialize with friends. While she will be strongly tempted use those sites for personal use, she needs to avoid putting her name on anything she would not want associated with her online image. If she wants to use social networking sites for personal use, she can create an alternate name which wouldn't be as easily tied to her which she could use to socialize.

Carol needs to remember the college student stereotype is not a stereotype that she should be promoting. Rather, she should focus on what her goals for the future are. If she wants to become a veterinarian, than she should be seen on veterinarian websites asking questions to gain knowledge and on animal rescue sites. If she is uncertain of her future goals, she can always find places where quality individuals should be seen, such as discussion boards for volunteer organizations.

USING SITES SPECIFIC TO YOUR GOAL

Certain sites may be very applicable to the goals you have for your online image. For instance, sites that are built to help people find true love will be helpful when you are trying to find true love. Often within sites like these you can create a profile. Within the profile section, you can add your website address. Your target audience is likely to be scouring those particular websites on the web. The target audience has an interest in finding people who match their needs and the best place to look for them is in a target rich environment.

To demonstrate this concept, consider Joe Smith, our HR executive who is looking for a new opportunity. Joe should attempt to get his online image on to HR professional sites. As an HR professional, Joe knows which sites he visits to look for executive talent. Joe has a distinct advantage. Joe knows the target audience very well, since most of the time Joe is part of the target audience.

In this case, Joe is on the other side of the process. Joe should also use sites which are frequented by executive recruiters. Joe knows what he looks for in an executive and should help executive recruiters see what they are looking for on these specific websites. Joe wants to be considered for job opportunities, so he also needs to use the websites built for those purposes. Joe should put his resume and links back to his website on job board websites like Monster.com.

HOW NOT TO ADD COMMENTS

As a word of caution, what you do not want to do is blanket the web with a generic comment that seemingly works for every location you decide to post your comments. This is the equivalent of spamming on the web and hoping that someone in your target audience is in the audience. While this may seem time effective to use the same comment over and over, what message would that send to your target audience? For instance, let's say you go out on the Internet and post the following message on multiple websites.

> *This product is by far the best of its class. None of the competition even compares. Out here in Springfield, USA, a person like me, John Jacob JingleHeimer-Schmitt, really can use this product. Not only was it easy to use, but it also solved a major problem for me. I can now sleep better at night knowing that this product has me covered.*

The above comment will get search engines to return your comment in search results. However, you wouldn't want this attributed to your online image. To be able to use it everywhere, the comment would need to be generic enough that what you have said could apply to any product. But when you write generic excrement like that, you aren't contributing anything of useful value. You are giving an endorsement, but not showing that you actually know what you are talking about. Since you are probably not a celebrity (otherwise you would want to be paid for an endorsement), few people could care less about your endorsement. People want to see substance, not an endorsement.

Alone, a single comment like the one above wouldn't hurt your online image, it just wouldn't help it either. However, compounded with multiple repetitive comments (even with slight variation) can do real damage to your online image. More importantly, what this type of mass commenting says to a target audience member is you either don't care how you appear online, do not carefully consider what you have to say, or worse, you take a one size fits all approach to everything you do. In any endeavor, showing that you have no insight, lack creativity, and/or are lazy rarely helps you achieve the opportunity you are looking for.

USING ELEMENTS OF YOUR ONLINE IMAGE THAT WERE ALREADY IN EXISTENCE

During the identification phase of Online Image Management, you identified pages and websites that constituted your online image at the time. Now, determine what information, if any, you want to use from that phase to help promote your new and improved online image. Go through the list that you created and find any potential referential elements of your online image. If you find information that will be of high worth, you may want to link to it from your website. For example, if I found a group roster from my past which I felt improved my online image, I would link to it from my website. Otherwise, if the old information on the Internet is useless but not damaging, you can leave it alone. Over time, those old elements of your online image will be replaced by the new elements of your online image. If you want to get rid of the information, removing information from the Internet is covered in the protection phase.

STEP 3 – USING THE LEMMING PRINCIPLE

While this step is in no means meant to be derogatory to lemmings (or people), it is simply meant to point out that people often go along with the group.   After all, if everyone else sees it one way, then it is likely that it is true.   You are not out to change the behavior of people, but rather, to use it to your advantage.   Having other people validate who you are strengthens your stereotype.

USING YOUR SOCIAL NETWORK TO YOUR ADVANTAGE

Associating yourself with professional people from your field will strengthen your online image.   During the conception phase you identified people within your social network that could help with the credibility of your stereotype.   Now is the time to use people within your social network which can be advantageous to use for your stereotype.   People who would be considered highly advantageous will be people that are recognized as a respected person by your target audience.   There is one slight caveat with this approach. If you are trying to look for Mr. Right, don't put links to any other potential Mrs. Right.

Use people within your social network which have a website or social networking profile which they control.   Without a presence on the Internet they can control, they have little means of helping promote your website.   What you will want to do is to have this person link to your website from their website or social networking profile. Have the person write up something which follows your stereotype. This person doesn't need to write anything more than a paragraph. The person should provide search terms that you are targeting, such as your name, e-mail address, your stereotype.   Additionally, when they link back to your website, have them use your name inside the link.   For example, if I wanted to link to my friend Mary, I might have a link that says "Check out Mary Trendsetter's website."

Let's use a fictional aspiring fashion designer named Mary Trendsetter as an example of how to use your social network. At this stage in her career, Mary has very few contacts in the fashion industry. Recognizing Mary's talent, several of Mary's professors from design school have offered to help Mary break into the industry in any way they can. Mary decides to ask her favorite professor if he could write a recommendation letter. In addition to writing it up in letter format, she has asked her professor to include the recommendation on his personal website. She also asks that he include her full name, location, web address, and e-mail address in the page. Mary explains her goals and why this will help her. Her professor agrees to help and offers to allow Mary the opportunity to review his recommendation which Mary accepts.

As Mary's professor works on putting the recommendation on his website, Mary asks a successful designer in the industry, a long time friend from school, to blog about Mary's latest design. Mary's friend agrees and asks that Mary reciprocate and blog about his newest design. Recognizing the win-win for both her online image and her friends, she agrees.

As Mary contacts various people in her social network, she is strengthening her online image. After a while, several of her contacts have write-ups about Mary on the Internet. Once the search engines find these references to Mary, these references will show up when someone searches for Mary. These references placed by multiple people all over the Internet build Mary's credibility as a fashion design expert.

If someone within your social network who can improve your online image does not have a website, you can help them by convincing them to go out and buy this book. Additionally, you can do a short write up on your website which will help their online image too. It's a win-win for both of you and let's be honest, me too.

USING VOLUNTEER ORGANIZATIONS THAT POST ROSTERS OF VOLUNTEERS

Being a volunteer has its own rewards. For starters, there is nothing like seeing the expression of happiness on someone else's face when you have helped them achieve something they would have had extreme difficulty doing on their own. It is true, we are happiest when we lose ourselves in the service of others. There are so many worthy causes out in the world that cannot survive without the constant help of volunteers. From Big Brothers/Big Sisters to the Red Cross, there is no shortage of opportunities to help.

But volunteer work may be able to help with your online image. Many organizations will put rosters or news releases out on the web. Finding ways for you to be included in rosters or news releases can help associate you with worthy causes. Being associated with these sorts of organizations improves your image as a quality human being.

When you are volunteering for your online image, make certain that the cause you are volunteering for will support your stereotype of being a quality individual. For instance, volunteering for a group like Habitat for Humanity which is universally seen positively, builds your stereotypes character. Conversely, a group which promotes genocide will not help you be seen as a quality individual.

If the organization which you volunteer for does not put rosters out on the Internet, you can always write about your experiences in your blog. Have someone take pictures of you in the act of volunteering. Be enthusiastic about your experiences in your blog. The last thing you need is to be complaining on the Internet about your work as a Big Sister.

USING THE RESOURCES AVAILABLE FROM YOUR EMPLOYER

Some of us have jobs that put our image out on the Internet for us. Often, employers will use a short biographical sketch along with any other pertinent information for their purposes. You should be able to modify what is being said about you on the corporate website. If the information that your employer puts out on the Internet supports your stereotype, build in keywords such as your full name and location into the information. Depending on the business, you may even be able to link to your own website. Furthermore, this type of resource should be linked to from your website if it supports your stereotype.

We will use Joe Smith, our HR director example, to illustrate this concept. On the corporate website, the company provides a short career history along with a professional picture of most of its senior management. The career history on the companies' website was written by Joe when he first started with the company almost 5 years ago. Since Joe is now focusing his online image, he has decided to rewrite the original career sketch so that he can improve its key terms and update the write-up. Joe includes his web address as well as elements of his stereotype that he is trying to promote. Once finished, he hands it over to the web team to update his web profile. Joe then turns to his own website. On his website, he adds a link to his career history on his employer's website from his online resume and his useful websites.

Joe was able to tie himself to his company, and show that his title that he claims on his resume is legitimate, as well as his career history. By placing a link on his website to this snippet on the corporate website, he is building his credibility by showing proof that he is what he says he is. Using his employer's website for this purpose was a great way to borrow the legitimacy of his company to establish his credibility.

SUMMING IT ALL UP

The ideas presented in this phase of Online Image Management should give you a started with promoting yourself. The concepts can be applied in every aspect of your online image and should be an opportunity for you to further strengthen your online image. Take the time, to carefully consider where you can place elements of your online image.

Be Patient. It takes time for the search engines of the world to scan websites for changes to their content. You will start showing up in the search results before you know it. Although your work will never be done with promoting your online image, you should not see it as a burden. Rather, recognize it as an amazing opportunity to let the world see who you are.

CHAPTER TEN

PROTECTION PHASE OF ONLINE IMAGE MANAGEMENT

"If you can't get rid of the skeleton in your closet, you'd best teach it to dance."

—William Shakespeare, English Playright

Your online image is your personal brand on the Internet. Protection of that brand needs to be vigorous. The process of Online Image Management has already helped you with the establishment and credibility of your online image. However, there will be threats to gaining and keeping the ground you have made. Threats will most likely come from other people who share your name, ex boyfriends or girlfriends and depending on your occupation, clients, coworkers, or customers.

This phase of Online Image Management is going to help you with the strengthening, prevention, and recovery aspects of Online Image Management. There are three threats you will want to deal with when protecting your online image: Your competition (namesakes), you, and people who want to tear you down.

STRENGTHENING METHODS FOR YOUR ONLINE IMAGE

We live in a world of six billion people and counting. That's six billion people and counting who all happen to have names which for the most part won't be unique. While you may be one of the lucky ones with a completely unique name, chances are you are not. These other people in the world which share your name, or namesakes, are your competition when it comes to ranking in the top 30 results. If you have a common name you are going to have to deal with multiple namesakes. Some names are so common you may have hundreds of people attempting to do the same things you are. Short of changing your name, you may be thinking you might as well give up. But wait, there is hope for you to remain in the top 30.

The methods outlined in the promotion phase of Online Image Management will strengthen the relevancy of your online image when search engines attempt to determine importance. One of the benefits of using the process of Online Image Management, is that you are already doing strong protection maneuvers for your online image. First by defining your message, you are being clear with who you are. Second, your stereotype helps paint a picture of you in their minds. Finally, you have been placing "marketing" messages all over the Internet to strengthen your online image. By continuing to do the activities in Online Image Management, you will further strengthen your online image.

Time is on your side as well. You will be getting into the Online Image Management before future generations have to pick up the scraps left over by the current generation. Having the time to make your online image stronger than the competition will make the protection of your online image a bit easier. You will have already made your online image prominent, all you have to do is maintain the ground you've gained by continuing the process of promotion phase of Online Image Management.

During the identification phase, you recorded pages which could be confused as you even though they were not. Now that you are familiar with the process of Online Image Management, you may be able recognize which of your namesakes are managing their online image.   There will be telltale signs in how they present themselves. If they present themselves in a professional manner, or they have a website dedicated to themselves, you will be able to recognize their efforts. If your namesake is aware of their online image, they are not likely to put garbage out on the Internet. The most they can do is put out conflicting information about you which hurts the clarity of your online image.

Keep in mind trying to beat out all the potential namesakes for rankings may not be worth extensive effort if you have an extremely common name.   During the promotion phase, you incorporate your online image into every communication with your target audience. This gives you the opportunity to educate them on how to recognize you. Because the person knows what to expect when looking for you, if something doesn't quite fit your stereotype, you may be not be confused with a namesake after all when all is said and done.

TACTICAL DOMAIN NAME REGISTRATION

If you want to strengthen your online image against namesakes, you can do so by registering multiple domain names. When it comes to search engine rankings, having your name appear in a URL carries an awful lot of weight. The more domains you control with your name in it will weaken the ability of your namesakes to find good domains. Registering domain names that could be potentially be used to steal your traffic away, is a great way to protect your online image.

You've already invested time and money into protecting your image. Take the opportunity to crush the opposition by purchasing protective domain names.   One of the best ways to protect your domain name is purchasing up similar domain names.   The strategy involved with tactical domain name registration is trying to register valuable domain names to you that would prevent someone from capitalizing on the effort you have made.

Before we get too far into this topic, you should have already maxed out your primary domain name registration for as long as possible. It makes little sense to purchase multiple domain names to protect one that you no longer own. If you haven't maxed the registration, please do so before purchasing other domains.

Registering more than one domain might feel like overkill (especially after you have maxed out the domain name registration) until you consider the alternative which is the weakening of your online image by people taking advantage of your hard work. An example of a company which registers variation of domain names to protect their online image is Google. Try going to gooogle.com (Yes, that's right, add the extra o.) You will be redirected to google.com. Now, take it a little further. Keep adding "o" to the Google name (e.g goooogle.com, goooooogle.com, gooooooogle.com and so on) and see how many people have registered variations of Google . What you will see is Google has purchased some of the variants while other companies wanting to capture some of Google's traffic have camped on with this type of variation.

While it is highly unlikely that you carry as big of a target as Google, the point is to illustrate the desire of individuals to confuse people into using their bogus domains. If Google had anticipated this early in the process they could have further strengthened their Internet presence, which is exactly what you can do.

Tactical domain name registration has benefits for everyone getting into website ownership including the personal website owner. For example, if you have a common name, registering multiple domains strengthens the likelihood that someone finds your website. Conversely, if your name is not that common, it gives you an opportunity to completely own the name on the Internet.   You could potentially be the only John Jacob Jinglehiemer Schmitt as far as the online community is concerned.

If you have already registered jjschmitt.com, you may want to consider purchasing the other domain and extension combinations. For example, check to see if, jjschmitt.net, jjschmitt.org jjschmitt.name are available. I would recommend that you stick with the common extensions.(.com, .net, .org, .name) and possibly the country domain extension (.us).

The next place to look for domains that would be valuable to you is the list of possible domain names you created in the build phase of Online Image Management. Review the domains in order of how desirable they appear to you. Once you have the ranking, you can go about purchasing as many domain names as you like.

Finally, try to purchase the common alternate spellings of you name.   For instance, the last name, Anderson is commonly spelled Andersen with an "e" instead of an "o". This common variation on the name might be the difference between someone finding you and some other John Andersen.   It will definitely be beneficial for people who, heaven forbid, use an alternate spelling.   While it is not possible to catch all the common misspellings, attempting to catch some would be a strong protection maneuver, especially after you become famous because of your website. You definitely won't want other people cashing in on your success.

The last element of tactical domain registration would be to register domain names for your children if you have them. It is only going to become more difficult to register a name as a domain names in the future. By registering domain names for your children, you will be able to secure their place for an online image in the 21st century. If their domain name is registered, you can always use backordering services to attempt to grab the domain quickly if it ever becomes available. Purchasing domains for your children will be a small investment, but will be worth every penny.

Only you can determine if tactical domain name registration is worth the cost and effort to you. I completely understand the annual ongoing costs of such registration strategies and would recommend to you doing only what makes sense to you.   If the most you can afford is to purchase nothing more than your primary domain name for a year then that is all you can do.

OUNCE OF PREVENTION

In popular culture, all of the focus with Online Image Management has been dealing with prevention of ruining your reputation and the consequences to your reputation. Countless news stories exist about how someone was punished for what they put on the Internet and why you need to be careful about what you put out on the Internet. Talk show hosts do their part by focusing on how to keep your kids safe. So why is there so much attention given to prevention of destruction of your online image?

There is a belief that once something is out on the Internet it's out there forever. While there is some truth to that belief it is not entirely true. For starters, it can be difficult, but not impossible, to remove content from the Internet. At the end of the day, the technology is run by people and people can control that technology. There are various methods to get the people who run the websites to remove content from their websites. So it is possible to get content removed from a website.

However, there is truth to the belief that once content is made publicly available in digital form it can be out there forever. Once the content has been accessible on the public domain of the Internet, it can be archived, saved, printed, or anything else you can do with an electronic document. For instance, if you allowed yourself to be photographed nude by an ex at any point in your life that didn't end well, you may have a problem. If this ex wants to get even with you those nude pictures may end up on the Internet as a way to get back at you. Now you should be concerned! Anyone who comes across your picture can save it to the hard drive of their computer. So even if you can get your ex to take it down, a stranger could repost it at any time. If your ex has so kindly named the file after you, your name is attached to every file that gets saved and reposted out there.

Once content is out of your hands and publicly available, it may never truly disappear. These nude pictures, showing your lapse in judgment, can reappear throughout time creating a potentially never ending cycle of image destruction, unless of course, you're totally hot. Just kidding. It's probably worse if you are totally hot because the pictures may never die. This is why you could say that it might be next to impossible to remove content from the Internet. This is why so much emphasis has been placed on prevention for your online image.

It is much simpler to keep your information off the Internet in the first place rather than trying to clean up the mess. It takes a bit of restraint and knowledge of what you are trying to do with your online image to make certain you don't put things out there that hurt your online image. With your online image you need to take the perspective that anything you put out on the Internet could exist forever.

Because of this perspective, you always need to keep your goals in mind when you put information on the Internet. You will not want to put anything out on the Internet that could jeopardize your online image in the long run. With web companies that archive everything they find, you may be able to remove something from being served on the Internet, but may never be able to truly get rid of something that should have never been there in the first place.

THE WEB 2.0 THREAT

Web 2.0 presents is a threat in which you need to protect yourself from you and your social network. Many of the activities of the previous phases have helped you take steps to protect your image. When you watch what you post on various message boards and only expose certain members of your social network, you are taking protective measures for your online image.

However, what do you do when you want to participate without regard to your online image? Using your name defeats the purpose of Online Image Management. The answer is simple. You create an alias which you can use to participate in the web 2.0 world. With this alias you can do whatever you like as long as you don't cross the line between your alias and your online image. It may go without saying, but never refer to this alias in your online image and do not mention your online image in your alias's world.

CREATING AN ALIAS OR ALTERNATE PERSONA

There are reasons why social networking websites have become so popular so quickly. Simply put, they are fun and a great way to connect with people. If you don't want to be burdened with trying to keep your socializing activities from interacting with your online image, there is a simple approach. Create an alternate persona of yourself which someone who was searching for your online image could not tie to you. Basically, if you can't be you, be somebody else. Think of it as an alias for you to participate in the discussions, blogging, and social networking websites.

Creating a different name for your alias would be the best way to hide out on the Internet. Even simple variations to a name such as a fancier spelling, hyphenating, or using a different first name can be all you need to create a different person. But why stop there? Your alias could be someone who lives in a different country, who does a job which you would never want to do.

Pay attention to the variation of the name that you decide to use. Some people may be attempting to manage their online image and you could be undoing all of their hard work. However, if you are going to create a different name, please search the Internet for that name before you settle on the alias name. The best practices would be to use a name that doesn't currently exist or a name that is so common that your persona would never make it in to the top 30.

Don't include your name or other types of information like your e-mail address that could tie the alias to your online image. Never cross the boundaries of an online image in any communication with a target audience member. Even if you think they are your "friend". Sometimes their duty to give full disclosure will supersede

your friendship. Or they may be a good friend who just doesn't realize what they are giving away when they forward that hilarious e-mail
you sent them from your alias account to the whole office.

     If you want to communicate via e-mail with friends, create an
alternate e-mail address which you could use to post on blogs and
other websites. Using a different e-mail address will keep your alias
from crossing the boundary into your online image by accident. You
can be as careful as humanly possible, but sometimes e-mails can be
posted on websites without your knowledge. When this happens, the
contents of your e-mail message will be exposed to the world as well
as your address and your alias's connection to you.

     However, sometimes when your best strengthening and pre-
ventative measures are not enough to prevent a cyber assassination
attempt, you will need to take measures to restore your good name.
Some people might just have it out for you and are willing to do whatever it takes to bring you down. If you are a victim of cyber assassination, there is no need to feel powerless to personal attacks made
against you over the Internet. There are several techniques you can
use to restore your online image ranging from asking nicely to taking
legal action.

RESTORATIVE METHODS

     Before moving into the fantastic world of Online Image Man-
agement, you may have already done a fair amount of damage to your
online image. In the identification phase of Online Image Management, you should have found anything that could be tied to you. You
should have identified the information that you would not want out on
the Internet. With this list in hand, you can get started removing this
information from the Internet.

DEALING WITH CYBER ASSASSINATION.

In the identification phase, you identified some likely people who could harm your online image. Some of those people on the list could act as a cyber assassin. When you researched your hit list, if you found that one of the people on your hit list has been publishing content about you and painting you in a bad light, your most likely course of action will be to respond.

Of the most tragic cases to deal with when you restore an online image are the cases of cyber assassination. Specifically, it is when people go out of their way to ruin your online image any way they can. People are often quite effective in their approach, because they are passionate about the subject matter. A cyber assassin is someone who feels they have been wronged in some fashion by the target of their assassination attempt.

Typically, a cyber assassin feels as if it their mission to "educate" everyone about how horrible their target is. Often the claims made by a cyber assassin are outright lies aimed at destroying the person's character. As you may know, it doesn't take much for a lie to be accepted as truth. While you may try to counter the claims, it is often an attempt in futility if the lie is repeated enough. However, having your side of the story out there isn't always bad idea if it is a bad enough accusation.

TWO APPROACHES TO REMOVING CONTENT

There are two approaches to removing content which could harm your online image. You can try to eliminate the content from existence altogether or you can make the content difficult to find. Either approach can be difficult to accomplish, yet both approaches are possible.

Before you embark on any restorative campaign, you should assess whether or not the content needs to be removed. Sometimes the information that you once considered damaging to your stereotype is not easy to connect to you. You were able to connect it to you because you know the content belongs to you. However, if you have a common name, it might not be easy for a person searching for information on you to associate the content with you. If all that is contained within the offending content is your name, with no other identifying characteristics, an average person who does not know you will not be able to conclusively tie the information to you or your online image.

If you need a complex search query to find the information, such as "Your name surfing buck naked" you should assess the likelihood of someone finding the information. Chances are, you were able to create the search terms because you know the subject of your search, you, best. As a general rule, if someone can find the offending information using the types of information you would find on a job or college application then you probably need to try to take care of the information.

Further, over time, the problem may correct itself. As you manage your online image, you will be adding content to the Internet. All of this content will eventually get indexed by the search engine companies. As a result, you may end up hiding whatever you found offensive simply by going through the process of Online Image Management.

REMOVING CONTENT FROM EXISTENCE

The effort to remove something from existence can be substantially higher than trying to make the content irrelevant by making certain it doesn't show up in the top 30 results. When you make the determination to remove the offending content from existence, you need to determine if it is worth the effort. You should ask yourself, "is this offensive material such that it would prevent me from reaching the goal of my online image?" If you determine that the content would impair your chances of achieving your goal, you will want to remove the content from existence. Otherwise, simply attempting to hide the content out of the top 30 search results may be enough to protect yourself.

Determining how to remove the content depends on the content you are trying to have removed. If you have control over the content, it is easier to get rid of the offending content. For instance, if a comment you wrote at some time in the past is posted on a news group or some such place, you can usually talk to the right people about getting it removed without much fuss.

However, if the offensive content is something you have absolutely no control over, you will have a more difficult time removing the offending content. Removing the offensive content may depend on if you are on good enough standing with the content owner. Typically, the author who wrote the content in the first place has the best capability to remove the content they wrote. The author of the content can usually log into the account where they created the content and remove it. If the author does not have access to remove the content then the author can contact the owner of the website and ask that the content be removed. Website owners are usually more accommodating to the creator of the content than they are to someone who simply doesn't like the content found on their site.

If you don't know who the content author is, you will need to find out who to contact to remove the content. You're going to need to contact a few people if you want to remove it completely. You can contact the owner of the website and the hosting company of the website if you want to have something removed which you do not control. All three players the author, the website owner, and the hosting company have different roles with which they can remove content. Finding ownership of the website can be as easy as performing a whois search on the domain name.

Using your favorite search engine, search for the term "domain name whois". This should provide you with a myriad of results which you can choose from. You are looking for a whois search which will allow you to find out the domain registration information. (By the way, whois searches are free, so don't pay someone to run the search for you.)

After performing the search on the domain you can find out who to contact to remove the content. You should be armed with a variety of contact information provided by the owner of the domain. All sites have to list the contact information when registering a domain, (Some people pay for a private registration, so you won't be able to get those contacts. For the most part people don't pay for private registration.) Starting with the administrative contact and working your way through the billing and technical contacts until you find someone who can respond to your request.

If the website with the offensive material is a website owned by a company i.e. Facebook, the website may list contact information which you could use to report abuse. Contacting the company which provided access for your cyber assassin can be your best bet to remove the content. The person who runs the website has complete control over the website.

Finally, if you can get the IP address of a website, you may be able to use the American Registry of Internet Numbers aka ARIN to find the contact information. To get the IP address of a website, you can use the Ping utility on a Windows based system. The Ping utility attempts to contact the website and will report back the IP address to you. To access ping, open a command window (prompt) and type "Ping websiteaddressgoeshere.com" . For example, if I wanted to find out the IP of WhooRu, I would go to the command prompt and type, "ping www.whooru.com" which would return the following text, "Pinging whooru.com [206.130.101.79] with 32 bytes of data:" The IP address is in the brackets. Additionally, you may want to check out some of the tools WhooRu offers to find this information.

When you contact someone to help you remove offensive comments be very clear as to why you want the material removed. If, for instance, you are dealing with an organization or company, they are ultimately the owner of the message. They can remove the content at their discretion. The better your case is to remove the content the more likely someone will be responsive. For instance, if your best argument for removing something from a website is "because I said so" you're likely to get nowhere. So, if you are attempting to remove the handiwork of a cyber assassin, outline all of the abuses of this cyber assassin.

It would be helpful if you found the agreements which anyone who uses the companies' services agree to. These are often referred to as "user agreements" or "terms of service". If you can find direct violations of user agreement, inform the company of the abuses by outlining the violations. If it is obvious why the content would be found offensive, a company which provides the hosting or website, will likely respond to your request to remove the content. After all, removing the content should be in the best interest of both you and the company involved.

You should try very hard to avoid making threats against this company. Remember, your problem with the content is ultimately between you and the content author. If you are getting nowhere talking to this person, take it to the next level. Find out who is in charge at the company and send a detailed letter outlining your experience with the company and what you would like them to do to remedy the situation. A nice touch would be to send the request in writing via certified letter. You will communicate the seriousness of your communication to them. Once you know they have received the letter, you can follow up with a phone call to verify they have, in fact, removed the offensive content.

If you are dealing with a private individual who is using hosting from a web hosting company you can contact the web hosting company and report the abuse. This maneuver will effectively take the knees out from under the website where the content is hosted. Free speech may be guaranteed in the United States and other countries around the world, but it is not the responsibility of the web host company who hosts the content to give the person who is defaming you online a forum to express that defamation. Likely, the content hosted on their servers is in violation with their terms of service agreement, between them and the website owner. The webhosting company will likely respond by terminating the account of the cyber assassin.   If they fail to remove the content, you could always tell them you are considering legal action to have the content removed.   Any web hosting company should be able to do the math and determine the $10 per month they are getting for hosting the persons content isn't worth involving a lawyer.

CONTACT SEARCH ENGINE COMPANY

Search engine companies have a mechanism in place to remove content which needs to be removed.   You will have to tell them why the offending page should be removed before they will be willing to comply.   Understand the search engine's purpose is to return appropriate results for search terms.   However, search engine companies are not in the business to restore your online image.   You may encounter some difficulty getting content removed unless the information out on the Internet would contribute to identity theft.   In these cases, search engines will usually work with you to de-list the material from their index.

TAKE LEGAL ACTION

Taking legal action should be considered the nuclear option when it comes to removing content from the Internet.   When other methods to get the content removed have failed, legal action may be your only course of action.   You can always take legal action against the individual, company, and/ or web hosting provider to remove the offensive content.   Consulting a lawyer will help you to know if you have a case before you take it to this step.   A lawyer will be able to determine if you have legal grounds for the removal of the offensive content.

In the now famous case of Sue Scheff vs. Carey Bock, Sue Scheff took Carey Bock to court over online defamation and won damages in excess of $11 million. Because this case is quite complicated and heated, I do not want to get into the merits of the case and who is right or wrong. It should serve as a warning of seriousness of online defamation or cyber assassination.

Don't get your hopes up, you probably are not going to get rich from online defamation unless someone like Bill Gates is going after you. But don't discount the legal option. It may be the single most effective way to take care of a cyber assassin who won't go away.

OBFUSCATION - THE ART OF MAKING THE CONTENT DIFFICULT TO FIND.

One of the ways you should be able to control offending content is to make it obscure. By having enough content on the web which will be returned when your name is searched for, you may be able to make the offending material disappear from the search engine results. Remembering that most people sift through the first 2 pages of search results, getting the website to rank lower in the search engine results is almost as good as removing the content altogether. The reason obfuscation is an art is because you are trying to manipulate search engine results. This is difficult to do because no one has a perfect understanding of how the search engines work other than the search engine companies.

While it may be useful to you to employ a company like Whoo-Ru, to help you obfuscate the offensive content, there is a technique you can use to make the offensive content disappear. Analyze the offending content for likely search terms which would return this content. Likely search terms would be unique terms such as your name or your location. Conversely, unlikely search terms would be common words or phrases which millions of web pages contain. Once you determine a list of terms which would return this content in a search, you can start targeting the terms or keywords.

To make the content obscure you need to work your targeted keywords into postings which you put out on the Internet. Using the techniques of the promotion phase, you should be able to put enough content out there to make the offensive content disappear. Placing content all over the Internet that happens to work in the keywords which you are targeting, should help you hide the offending content.

The difficulty of making the content obscure, is you are dependent on someone searching for you based on the keywords that you target. Unfortunately, you will probably not be able to anticipate all of the different ways that a person could search for you, thus making it difficult to truly hide this page.

Remember that search engines take time to update their index, it may take a while for you to see the fruits of your efforts. Keep at it and within the space of a couple months you should be happy with your results.

FIGHTING FIRE WITH FIRE

If you cannot get rid of the material on the Internet, you may want to consider responding to accusations on your website. You should only do this if the cyber assassin has managed to destroy your online image. Only you will know if you are suffering a loss from the accusations made by your cyber assassin. However, if you have had multiple people inquire about the accusations, it should be a strong indicator to you that the cyber assassin has been successful.

Responding to accusations is acceptable within the bounds of your website. But, it may draw unnecessary attention to the issue when someone might not have known about it. Consult with a lawyer before you respond on your website if you plan on pressing a lawsuit.

If you respond it may be as simple as stating that a lawsuit is pending.

Some people will take it a step further and create content on the Internet to discredit their cyber assassin. It is an approach you can take as long as you are truthful in your counter attack. You would not want to be sued in the process. I don't recommend this approach because I believe that if you set out to destroy someone you ultimately destroy who you are in the process.

Another maneuver which some people will use to remove content will involve hiring a search engine optimization company, like WhooRu, which specializes in restoring your reputation. While this may be effective, you should investigate how any company eliminates content. Some reputation management companies have built a business using any tactic they can find to manipulate search engine results. Sometimes, these tactics are referred to as black hat SEO techniques. Generally, black hat tactics are often deemed unethical even though they are effective. Search engine companies like Google will often black list companies which use black hat tactics. Worst yet, if the search engine company determines that the reputation management company has violated the search engine's terms of service, they will ban the website and all of the verifiable clients of that company.

Ask the reputation management company for a list of the tactics they use and then search for each tactic name along with the term "black hat". If this tactic is listed as a black hat tactic you may want to consider using a different company

SUMMING IT ALL UP

Next to the creation of your online image, the protection of your online image is essential to Online Image Management. Your online image is who you are on the Internet and increasingly it is the equivalent of who you are in real life. Be proactive in protecting yourself and responding to threats as they appear.

CHAPTER ELEVEN

MAINTENANCE PHASE OF ONLINE IMAGE MANAGEMENT

"What we hope ever to do with ease, we must learn first to do with diligence."

—Samuel Johnson, English Author

Think of this phase as the owner's manual for your newly crafted online image — complete with scheduled maintenance and how to take care of your online image over time. Now that you have equipped yourself with an online image, you need to learn how to take care of your online image.

The Internet is constantly evolving and you need to be adaptive to the changes you encounter. Consider how quickly a website can become mainstream and change the face of the Internet. It wasn't that long ago in 2003 that MySpace opened its doors for business and changed the way that many people socialize. YouTube is another massive example of the changing social networking landscape of the Internet. Within a year of its launch in December 2005, YouTube was so popular that Google bought it for $1.65 billion. With YouTube on the scene, video sharing is now mainstream.

Knowing when to revisit the phases of your online image can help you deal with the constantly evolving Internet.   While the promotion phase needs to be done all the time, other phases need to be done periodically.   Some of the phases will be triggered by specific events, and others will be revisited as needed.

Next, using trends can help maintain and strengthen your online image.   With all trends, there are good and bad things about trends.   Trends such as blogging or using Twitter have caught on very rapidly.   Knowing which trends to latch on to and which trends to pass by will be an important skill for managing your online image.   Furthermore, there are tools that you have available to help you monitor how your online image is being utilized.   You will learn about some tools which you can use to see what people are doing on your blog as well as how to use search engines to check up on your online image from time to time.

Finally, in this phase you will learn how to evolve your identity over time.   You may want to be Casanova today, but tomorrow you may want to be a CEO.   Knowing how to tackle the challenge of removing one stereotype and replacing it with another can help you as your online image adapts to your changing needs.

IDENTIFYING TRENDS

Always be on the lookout for trends and ways the Internet can help you further strengthen your online image.   Watching for particular trends on the Internet will help you take advantage of trends which could help your online image.   With Online Image Management, there are three types of trends you need to watch out for on the Internet: trends your stereotype should know about, trends of socialization technology, and trends of how to present content.

As you evaluate trends and technology, you will need to determine when it makes sense to join the trend or use the technology. Early adaptors of technology are people that jump on the latest and greatest technology.   While you don't need to be an early adaptor to new technologies, make sure you are there when the technology goes mainstream.   While sometimes reaping the benefits of being able to take advantage of really cool technology, early adapters often jump too early into the new technology.   Despite how promising a technology is, there is always a downside to getting involved early.   New technology has not had the time to have all the kinks worked out and lacks the full feature support of a mature, time tested technology.   Furthermore, new technology can and often fails early in the process due to lack of interest in the technology community.

There are benefits to jumping on a technology early in its life cycle.   You can be more advanced than the competition because it is something that not many people have seen or used themselves.   You will be able to present yourself in an interesting and advanced fashion. While there are benefits to early adoption, there is a downside to early adoption of technology and trends.   To illustrate the pros and cons with early adoption, think of the industry battle to decide the next generation DVD format.

The current format for the standard DVD lacked the storage capacity necessary to store the information needed to display movies in high definition.   A new format was needed with additional storage space.   There were two camps in the battle, the Blu-ray camp and the HD-DVD camp.   While there were pros and cons to each of the technologies, both technologies solved the problem of providing a high definition experience.   Early adaptors of both of the technologies enjoyed the high definition DVD format while most people were still watching their standard DVD's.   Yet, the early adaptors of the technologies struggled through changing specification for the technologies as well as the high cost and limited selection of movies and players.   In the end, the Blu-ray technology won the battle for the next generation DVD format.   When the dust settled, people who bought into the Blu-ray format were pretty happy with their decision.   While conversely, the people who had bought into the HD-DVD, probably cringed when this topic was brought up.

The most effective choice for a consumer wanting to take advantage of the HD-DVD format was to wait until the standard technology had been accepted by the industry.   Once the format standard was decided, the entire industry could get behind the one format, effectively increasing competition and lowering cost for the consumer.

When it comes to Online Image Management and adoption of technology and/or trends, its best to wait until an industry moves in the direction so that you don't get burned by a wrong decision.   However, always consider the value to your online image when you make a decision to adopt the technology.   If you think it will help your stereotype to be at the forefront of an emerging technology, then by all means adopt that technology.   If you do get burned by a wrong decision, you can make it right by backing off the changes you made to support that technology.

The safest bet as to when to adopt a new technology as it has gone mainstream.   After the technology has been out for a while, usually a year, you will be able to judge what people think of the technology.   Determining what people think of a technology is as simple as searching for the technologies' name and the word review, e.g., ("YouTube Review").   When you read the review, pay attention to the negatives of the technology.   If the negatives refer to social stigma terms, such as "a site for teenagers" or "shouldn't let your children on this site", you probably won't want to take advantage of the technology.   The stereotype of the technology, in this case, can influence your online image.

TRENDS WHICH YOUR STEREOTYPE SHOULD BE RESPONSIVE

It would be hard to argue that a person should avoid emerging trends in their field. In fact, many people attempt to stay up to date with the latest lingo in their field. This concept is often referred to as being buzzword compliant. A buzzword is a trendy word or phrase which generates buzz or discussion about the latest and greatest thinking in the field. Every industry has buzzwords such as technologies or ideas which everyone is talking about. In the weight loss industry, a few years back the South Beach diet would have been a buzzword. At the time, telling people you were trying the South Beach diet would have communicated that you stayed on top of the trends in the dieting world.

Your stereotype should be responsive to the buzzword trends within your stereotype's field. For instance, if you have promoted your stereotype as an educator, your stereotype should be able to reflect trends in the education industry. Furthermore, being up to date within a chosen field is a quality characteristic of any individual. Letting people know that you are up to date shows that you care about your field enough to stay at the forefront of the discussion.

TRENDS OF SOCIALIZATION TECHNOLOGY

Watching what becomes popular on the Internet to socialize can be another way to improve your online image. Taking advantage of new ways to socialize will allow you to present your online image over the Internet in areas which will allow you to promote your online image.

Some socialization technologies have hit the ground running. YouTube, for example, has been one of those game changing technologies that have come online in recent years. Within a year of its launch, it was already a part of popular culture. YouTube has changed the way we view sharing content with each other over the Internet. After all, where else can you see videos of people making complete fools of themselves anytime you want.

We are all still learning how to interact with a technology like YouTube. Companies are starting to take advantage of the free bandwidth and access to a prime market of individuals. Companies are putting their music videos, movie trailers, and product demonstra-tions on YouTube. Many individuals are using YouTube to launch their careers. As an online image manager, YouTube provides a way to put streaming video on your website without the hassle which would have previously accompanied putting video on a website.

Yet, not all socialization technology will make sense to utilize for promotion an online image. For example, gaming companies allow the ability to chat and to socialize through the game features. While fun and useful to chat while playing your favorite shoot 'em up games, chances are search engines will not be able to index the chat transcripts and you likely wouldn't want to be associated with online gaming. That is, of course, unless being associated with the gaming site would improve your online image.

Choosing socialization technologies makes sense when it will improve your online image. You know what you are trying to do on the Internet better than anyone. If you can use the latest and great-est virtual reality world to better promote yourself then do it. Just remember to look into the ramifications before you leap into any new technology.

TRENDS OF HOW TO PRESENT CONTENT

As an online image manager, you need to be aware of how to present content with the website design, the website structure, content presentation format, and the layout of the content. For the most part if you like the way something is presented over the web, you should try to pick it apart and find out why. Maybe you like the way the text is written, or maybe it's as simple as you like the subject matter. Learning why you like something can help you identify what communicates effectively with you.

Once you figure out exactly what you like, try applying it to elements of your online image. If it communicates better you should leave it in, otherwise if it makes things more confusing then revert back to what you had previously. Before you do anything drastic, get some opinions about how well your new design communicates. When it comes to design, the more opinions you can get on the matter, the better feel you will have for the ability of your design to communicate.

When you see enough people using the same elements of design, that would be considered a trend. Website design, like every field of design, is a trendy business. What in vogue today will be ridiculed tomorrow in the web design world. Keeping up with design trends can be maddening. So unless your stereotype needs to be seen as a trendy, you shouldn't need to update your design frequently with every trend.

Unless you have an eye for design, trends in design might not be as easy to determine. If you want to spot web design trends, the easiest way to spot trends is to visit web designer websites. Many designers tend to follow the crowd when it comes to design. After looking at the portfolios of several designers, you should start to notice common elements such as the focusing on particular colors, (pastels, earth tones, etc.) and placement of the menu structures.(left, right, top, middle, bottom).

Even though your website lives in a world obsessed with design, you should be focused on presentation of the content. Primarily, in the design world, presentation affects the way people comprehend content. A poor presentation of content will distract the reader from the message of your content. For instance, if you have red text on a black background it will be difficult to read the text. In contrast, well presented content will deliver the message of your content so there is no ambiguity and no distractions to the message. As a result of the importance of presentation, online image managers should always be on the lookout to find better ways to present their content. When you evaluate a new way to present your content you should always ask whether or not the new way makes your content easier to understand. If the new approach improves the communication of your stereotype, then as an online image manager you should use the technique.

Although you do not need to be responsive to web design

trends, there is a wide held expectation that a website's design changes from time to time. There are a number of reasons why this is the case. Over time, newer Internet browsers give designers additional capabilities to design their websites. Additionally, Internet users who have been on the web for a while are familiar with companies changing the appearance of their websites from time to time to add features or "enhance" the experience of their customers. Furthermore, a design change is considered freshening up the appearance of a website, often communicating that the website is fresh, improved, and well maintained.

When your website begins to look as out of date as the Brady Bunch's home it might be time to consider redesigning your website. Unfortunately, the antiquated look doesn't work as well as it does in the real world. Many people don't see a charming old web site, rather they see a website that nobody cares to keep up. Of course it will be dependent on what you can afford, but revamping your website is a good way to communicate that you take care of your website. Updating the look of your website is the equivalent of putting on new siding on your home. While it is not something you do frequently, you do it when it is necessary to look like you are current. However, choosing to change the look of your content should only be done when it is an improvement to your existing online image.

MONITORING YOUR ONLINE IMAGE

Monitoring is a crucial element of the maintenance phase of Online Image Management. In order to be responsive to challenges to your online image, you need to know what is happening to your online image. During the maintenance phase of Online Image Management, you should be periodically tracking the performance of your online image when you do certain searches. The terms you are going to want to track over time were the terms you searched for your online image with during the identification phase.   For example, your name, your e-mail, and your address are all terms you will want to track to see how you appear on the Internet.   This type of monitoring will help you figure out whether or not you are successful with your attempts to do Online Image Management.   Performing the search for your on-line image on a monthly basis, will let you see the fruits of your labor. As you perform the search, record every page which belongs to you and its ranking for the particular search.   For instance, if your website URL comes up 1st on the search results, record the URL, the term you searched for, and its #1 ranking.

MONITORING YOUR SOCIAL NETWORK

Your social network is another area to monitor.   You can do this in a number of ways, including the hitlist searching that you did during the identification phase of Online Image Management.   Per-forming these searches on a frequent basis, such as four times a year with the changing seasons, is a good way to keep tabs on whether or not someone has emerged as an Internet author.

A surprisingly effective way is to ask members of your social network if they have a blog or maintain their online image.   This will be a quick way to find out if they maintain a presence rather than hav-ing to track it down yourself.

If you can convince someone to take control of their online image, they are less likely to put something out on the Internet which could hurt your online image.

USING SITE STATISTICS

When you contracted with the web designer to build your site you should have asked that a website statistics package be installed so you can keep track of the traffic coming to your web site. If you didn't get this feature, your web hosting provider should be able to help set up site statistics for your website. Assuming that you have a website statistics package, a website statistics program can analyze the traffic to your website. Take the time to get familiar with your website statistics software. It is your window into how your website is communicating with the world. You should be able to learn about what people do on your websites, such as which topics they visit. Knowing this information can let you know which topics are very interesting and which ones aren't drawing people. Once you can see a problem, it's a lot easier to address.

If you see that some of your areas on your website aren't getting much traffic, you can try to make it more interesting. Changing the topic language may help draw people into the topic. For example, a topic named "what I did last summer" could be renamed "My Summer in Cambodia" or "Building wells in the 3rd world". Many packages are able to tell who came to your website in terms of geographic location, and the Internet address the visitor came from. You might be able to see if a particular employer is checking out your online image or if a university where you are applying to med school has been by your online image. Knowing this information may tell you whether or not you have been successful at drawing your target audience.

A word of warning, don't rely on statistics too much when it comes to identifying where people came from. People get to the Internet in a variety of ways, such as from home or from work. When they connect to your website they will show up as having come from different locations even though it is the same person. If you don't see your targeted audience show up, don't be discouraged. As long as you are getting traffic to your website, your online image is being seen.

Additionally, you should be able to see the keywords and phrases people used in searching for your website. Although limited, you should be able to draw some valuable information from the terms people used to find you. Ideally, you will see your name along with some other targeted keywords show up in the site statistics.

WHEN TO REPEAT THE PHASES.

Knowing when to revisit the phases is a vital component to understanding how to manage your online image. Since your online image is a reflection of who you are, your online image needs to adapt as your needs for your online image change. Some of the phases need to be done continuously, while other phases will be evoked as needed. In general, phases which you do all the time are intended for the promotion and protection of your online image. Other phases are revisited when events occur that warrant action on your part.

PHASES WHICH YOU DO ALL THE TIME.

The maintenance phase, as well as the promotion phase should be done all the time. The maintenance phase is there to help you manage your online image so it should be clear that it is a phase which is intended to be used all the time. The maintenance phase includes an element of monitoring, which needs to be done on a frequent basis.

The promotion phase helps you build your online image. Adding elements of your online image to the Internet is something which can help you improve your online image as time marches on. Continuously promoting yourself will, in the long run, allow you to maintain a secure foothold on your online image.

The element of prevention in the protection phase, should always be done on an ongoing basis as well.   It should be at the forefront of your online image thoughts.   You will not want to jeopardize your hard work by making a mistake which will haunt you.

PHASES YOU SHOULD DO PERIODICALLY

Knowing where you stand on the Internet and how your online image is performing is important when it comes to Online Image Management.   The entire identification phase should be something you redo at least annually and at the most every six months. If you are a person who is fairly stable with your goals, annually should be a sufficient amount of time to check in on your goal for your online image. However, if you are someone who changes their goals in life as quickly as you change your clothing then you should consider reviewing your online image as often as every six months.   You will be able to tell whether or not your stereotype supports your goals by checking up on it. If you find that you can't decide on a goal for your online image that lasts for six months, focus on presenting yourself as the stereotype for a quality individual and leave your online image as that until you decide on a goal that is going to stick.

PHASES YOU SHOULD DO AS NEEDED

The identification phase and monitoring element of the maintenance phase will let you know when you need to kick off the phases which should be done as necessary. While you can revisit any of the phases any time you want, there are times when you will need to revisit a phase because of something you uncover. The conception phase, build phase, and protection phase should be done when they are called for based on what you find when you identify and or monitor your online image. For example, if you find a disturbing page show up in your search results, you will need to start up the protection phase.

An event which would trigger action on your part would be if you were to determine that you need to modify your online image or update the design of your website to improve your stereotype. In that scenario, you would want to evoke the conception and build phases of Online Image Management. Other events, like finding questionable content on the Internet which reflects badly for your online image, will make you want to revisit the restoration step of the protection phase.

EVOLVING YOUR ONLINE IMAGE

Life is all about change. We are constantly bombarded with change every day. Some change is positive and some change can be quite bad for us. Regardless of the type of change, it helps us to grow which in turn causes us to adapt and evolve. As you evolve, your goals in your life might change. If your goal for your online image changes, you will want to evolve your online image.

Once you determine that it is time to evolve your online image, you will need to see how similar your new goal is to your prior goal. Sometimes your new goal is a natural extension of your prior goal. For instance, you may have wanted to be the lead designer for an interior decorating firm when you created your online image. Once you have realized that goal, you may realize that you want to take the next step and run your own interior decorating company. The stereotype to run your own interior decorating company and the stereotype

ness owner who is God's gift to interior design.

When your new stereotype is very similar to your old stereotype, changing your online image may be very straightforward. Transforming elements of your online image to support your new stereotype may be accomplished with relative ease. Modifications to the content and structure of your website, as well as a slightly different message, may be all you need to do to change stereotypes.

Other times, your new goal for your online image is the polar opposite of your prior goal. As an example, let's assume that you are an accountant and have been portraying yourself as a down to earth, numbers oriented, no personality, accountant. For some reason, one day you decide it's time to pursue your dreams of being a rock star. While you see this as a natural extension of who you are, no one on the Internet will see you as a rock star.

It simply doesn't make sense to see a rock star/ accountant stereotype unless that is part of your gimmick. In this case, you will need to start over. Fortunately, you can save some time, some elements of your prior online image may be able to be incorporated into your new online image. For instance, you already own the domain name you need to manage your online identity. However, a new design would be in order as well as new content, topics, and structure. Further, your promotional efforts will break a good majority of the rules of writing content. After all, rock stars don't play by the same rules as the rest of us do.

Additionally, when you drastically change stereotype, you may need to go after your prior stereotype with the same zeal as if you were dealing with a cyber assassination attempt. Using the protection phase to remove a past stereotype may be easier than you think. Since you are the author of the content that has been placed out on the Internet, people should be fairly responsive to your desire to have it removed.

By going through the identification and conception phases of help you do the necessary gap analysis of where you are and where you want to be.   Once you perform the analysis, you can make the determination of which of the remaining phases need to be performed.

SUMMING IT ALL UP

Your online image is with you for life. If you treat your online image well by maintaining it and improving it over the years, it will help you achieve your goals. Remember that you are in the driver's seat when it comes to your online image. You are the one who knows best how to present yourself on the Internet.

FINAL THOUGHTS ON ONLINE IMAGE MANAGEMENT

"You can't escape the responsibility of tomorrow by evading it today."

—*Abraham Lincoln, American President*

Who knows what the future will bring. Of course, no one — not even me — can say for certain that people will continue to use the Internet like they do today. But if I were a gambling man, I wouldn't bet that people are going to magically start respecting each other's privacy online. Our inherent curiosity will always draw us to the Internet because of its capacity to fill that need.

Throughout the book I've reiterated how the critical social skill of the 21st century will be Online Image Management. Hopefully, now you see how important it is to manage your online image and why it is necessary to do so. It is my hope that you will prepare to take advantage of the opportunities the Internet is presenting.

I don't know about you, but I am optimistic about the future and what the Internet will continue to bring. Especially, when it comes to Online Image Management. One thing is for certain: we are in this together. All of us will be impacted by the social implications of the Internet. And together, we will learn how to live with the Internet being part of our lives.

So as I end this book, I wish to leave you with one final quote from the 100 B.C. era Roman philosopher, Marcus Tullius Cicero. "Tomorrow will give us something to think about."